LINCOLN CHRISTIAN COLLEGE

PREACHING IN TODAY'S WORLD

PREACHING IN TODAY'S WORLD

JAMES C. BARRY

Compiler

BROADMAN PRESS
Nashville, Tennessee

© Copyright 1984 • Broadman Press

All rights reserved

4221-13

ISBN: 0-8054-2113-0

Dewey Decimal Classification: 251

Subject Heading: PREACHING / / SERMONS

Library of Congress Catalog Card Number: 83-24021

Printed in the United States of America

Unless otherwise noted, Scripture quotations are from the King James Version of the Bible.
Scripture quotations marked (GNB) are from the *Good News Bible*, the Bible in Today's English Version. Old Testament: Copyright © American Bible Society 1976; New Testament: Copyright © American Bible Society 1966, 1971, 1976. Used by permission.
Alton H. McEachern, "Narrative Preaching: Telling the Story" is adapted from McEachern, *Dramatic Monologue Preaching* (Nashville: Broadman Press, 1984).
Alton H. McEachern, "The Distant Disciple—Nicodemus" appeared in *Proclaim*, July 1974.

Library of Congress Cataloging in Publication Data
Main entry under title:

Preaching in today's world.

  Bibliography: p.
  1. Preaching—Addresses, essays, lectures.
2. Sermons, American.   I. Barry, James C., 1920-
BV4222.P65   1984   251   83-24021
ISBN 0-8054-2113-0 (pbk.)

Contents

Introduction
Preaching in Today's World
James C. Barry

"The voice of one crying in the wilderness" (John 1:23). The demands of contemporary preaching are such that one can understand the emotions of the prophet Isaiah or of John the Baptizer. The frustrations and challenges of preaching week after week force the conscientious pastor to fall back constantly on the promises of God. The wildernesses of contemporary society continue to offer their uncertainties and their risks around every bend in the pastoral road. Pity the pastor, however, who allows these problems to overshadow the joy and beauty that can be found along the same way.

Difficult and challenging as preaching in today's world may be, it remains central to the cause of the kingdom of God, to the health of the church, and to the fulfillment of the minister. In many circles it continues to be the watermark for measuring effectiveness in ministry. And, when going gets rough, it can still be undergirded by the same power that the apostle Paul found adequate in the first century.

All efforts to list criteria for measuring effectiveness in preaching today end in some degree of frustration. What seems to work with one person finds limited success with another. Principles related to the preparation and delivery of sermons are heard, learned, and practiced by two preachers from the same preaching class, using the same biblical text. One congregation hears the sermon gladly and is moved to action; the other is left wishing for something more relevant.

The personal and intangible elements in preaching continue to outweigh the technical when it comes to measuring spiritual impact on the total person. However, these elements are totally compatible,

7

for one can preach with deep convictions concerning God, the Bible, the church, and other biblical themes with full integrity and, at the same time, be technically correct homiletically.

In an effort to evaluate and to enrich contemporary preaching, a group of creative, concerned pastors gathered in Atlanta, Georgia, for three days to share ideas that were in the forefront of their thinking about preaching. Ten persons prepared papers to present to the group. These papers served as the basis for an extended discussion on the subjects.

These papers created sufficient interest among other persons that publication was requested. Another suggestion was that a sermon be included with each paper to illustrate the central thrust of the paper. The sermons were preached in a regular Sunday worship service by the author. These papers and the companion sermons make up the following chapters of this book.

The book opens with a paper on "Preaching to the Contemporary Mind" by David Matthews. He illustrates the difficulty of defining the contemporary mind and the mind changes from one generation to another. He offers four characteristics of the contemporary mind in noting that: (1) it is both secular and religious; (2) it strives for simplicity; (3) it distrusts words; and (4) it is accustomed to quality media of communication. He concludes by saying that much preaching fails to reach the contemporary mind because it is not adequately grounded in divine truth—"What is most truly new, what is most genuinely contemporary, contains within it what is most old . . . the Word of God . . . because it is eternal."

Humility is almost a lost note in contemporary society. This may be the reason David Matthews has chosen to illustrate his chapter with the sermon "On Being Humble." He suggests that the spirit of humility is central to the faith of a Christian in any age.

Calvin Miller provides some unusual insights on motives and actions related to preaching and church growth in his chapter. In keeping with his usual creative style of writing and speaking, he evaluates both biblical and contemporary efforts to reach people through preaching and other methods. In very subtle ways, he helps the reader to see some of the flaws in widely accepted practices in preaching. His tongue-in-cheek comments about success in ministry leave one with a strange mixture of smiles and tears . . . of hope and sadness. Miller compares the artistry of preaching as found in the Chrysostoms, the Maclarens, and the Fosdicks with the zeal of the Jonahs, the Whitefields, and the Billy Sundays. He speaks at length concerning the relationship of the sermon to the growth of a church and to biblical authority. This is one chapter that the reader may need to go over more than once before grasping all the possible nuances of many statements.

The sermon for chapter 2 is provided by J. Truett Gannon, who was the facilitator of discussion on this subject. Gannon is the pastor of the rapidly growing Smoke Rise Baptist Church of Stone Mountain, Georgia.

Through his book, *The Teaching of the Parables,* Peter Rhea Jones has become a recognized interpreter of the parables. Thus, this chapter on "Parabolic Preaching: Perspectives on Life" is a welcomed addition to the resources a pastor needs in preaching on these stories from the Old and New Testaments. Jones contends that the parables provide a powerful and compelling illumination of contemporary life. Busy pastors will find his suggestions for sermon series a helpful guide in grouping the parables for preaching. For example, he suggests a series on the seed parables, the householder parables, the evangelistic parables, and many others.

His sermon "The Compassionate Samaritan" is a good illustration of how a biblical incident can offer a powerful perspective on contemporary life. For Jones the parable in Luke 10:25-37 paints two revealing pictures: (1) a picture that exposes invalid and inauthentic religion—the religion of two churchmen; and (2) a picture that extols authentic religion—the genuine religion of a compassionate Samaritan.

Confessional preaching and John Claypool are often thought of together by those who work in the fields of homiletics. He has modeled for other preachers a method of preaching that can be used by all preachers occasionally to enrich their preaching. Claypool tells how this method evolved in his ministry and then makes some observations concerning the method—both positive and negative.

His three positive conclusions are: (1) Jesus taught it; (2) Paul utilized it; and (3) it is true to the incarnational principle. He warns of obvious dangers and potential weaknesses. These come into view when two questions are asked: (1) what is my motive? and (2) what is the likely consequence of such an action?

The sermon by John Claypool, "Slow Learners and Hope," is an excellent illustration of the method he has discussed in his paper.

In his paper "Ethical Dimensions of Preaching," Cecil Sherman outlines some of his objectives relative to his ministry at the First Baptist Church of Asheville, North Carolina. He is not as concerned about building an acceptable checklist of sermons on various subjects as he is about amending the way his people think and live. His goal is to lead his people to become like the God they worship. He illustrates at length that ethical preaching is basic to the gospel. Also, he feels that ethical preaching helps the pastor in his efforts to move his people along the process from paganism to grace. Further, ethical preaching will help the pastor minister to the total person, so that believing and behaving will be companions along the Way.

The story of the pharisee and the tax collector has been chosen as the basis of a sermon on Christian ethics. In this sermon, Sherman clarifies what he means by the lifelong process of growth from paganism to grace. This is an idea that every minister can use often.

"Legitimate Shortcuts in Sermon Preparation" by Lavonn Brown will probably be the most practical paper in the book for the average pastor. Brown is very honest in noting some of the not-so-legitimate shortcuts to preaching, such as the "Saturday Night Special." However, he offers an abundance of ideas for sermons and for sermon series that will leave the average preacher "suffering from an embarrassment of riches where sermon ideas and texts are concerned." Also, he provides ample resources for developing the ideas suggested.

The sermon used to illustrate a shortcut in preaching is entitled "Bloom Where You're Planted." This is a good example of narrative preaching and models for the minister what he can do with many other biblical personalities and incidents.

One of the most challenging ideas facing ministers today is found

in "Coordinating Preaching with Church Objectives." William Hull
is bold to suggest a unified approach to ministry, not only for the
pastor but also for pastor and people and all the ministries they
perform. He provides a strong biblical base for the concept that all
are the people of God and that all should participate in a shared
ministry. This includes the preaching, with the purposes undergirding this paralleling the purposes of the people of God. The sermon
beckons and propels the people of God toward the fulfillment of
their mission here on earth. Hull outlines the six major objectives
around which the First Baptist Church of Shreveport, Louisiana,
have organized their ministries. These are worship, outreach,
nurture, fellowship, service, and support. Their emphasis on the
priesthood of all believers has started them in the direction of
sharing in the ministries related to all of these objectives.

The idea that every member is a minister has been accepted in
theory only, if at all, by the average church member. Hull tries to
change this limited understanding with his sermon "Your Place in
Your Church." It provides both information and motivation for the
members to become a part of the ministry of their church.

"Narrative Preaching" by Alton McEachern stresses the great
need for preaching not only to be biblical but also contemporary. He
calls on preachers to present familiar biblical truths through new
and fresh methods. McEachern notes that much of the Bible was
first presented in story form. Many of the writers of the Bible were
master storytellers, as was Jesus. He goes on to say that a well-told
story still has great appeal for all age groups. His "How-to" section of
the chapter will have special appeal for those who have not tried
narrative preaching.

The sermon illustration of narrative preaching is in the form of a
dramatic monologue on the New Testament personality Nicodemus.
It is an excellent example of first-person preaching.

If one is to preach in today's world, he will preach in the context of
crises. This is the theme of the chapter by Altus Newell. How does
sudden congregational grief influence the content of the sermon,
and how does the sermon minister to the people in the midst of
grief? Newell shares some personal experiences that speak to these

questions, and he offers some guiding principles that will help keep all of life in proper perspective. He suggests a program of preaching in response to congregational crisis that includes four phases: (1) the nature and mission of the church faced with crises; (2) crisis response in the life of Christ; (3) other biblical models for crisis response; and (4) response to questions about the nature of God. A series of sermons was suggested for each phase.

The sermon "Thy Will Be Done" speaks to a question most often asked in times of crises, Did God will for this to happen? Here Newell speaks of: (1) the intentional will of God; (2) the circumstantial or permissive will of God; and (3) the redemptive will of God.

If preaching is truly Christian, it will be done in the context of worship. However, this has not been the thinking of many who cry out for the centrality of preaching. Thus, Robert Bailey, in "Preaching in the Context of Worship," provides a careful overview of the relationship of preaching and worship. In spite of what some preachers may have done to play down all that came before the sermon or that which may be tacked on at the end, Bailey tells us no conflict should exist between preaching and other elements of worship. He encourages worship planners to work simultaneously on preaching and worship so that each will compliment and support the other. Where there is unity in the total service, the impact upon the congregation is usually greater. A number of suggestions for involving laypersons in the worship services can be found in this chapter.

What do people expect to happen when they gather for worship? In his sermon "The Emptiness of Wrong Expectations," Robert Bailey helps his audience to see the hurt that can come with wrong expectations as well as the fulfillment that may come with the right. The sermon includes a number of strong illustrations.

A brief, annotated bibliography related to the emphases of this book is included. William Tuck prepared this, not as an extensive bibliography on preaching, but to offer suggestions for extended reading on the subjects discussed.

In addition to the persons whose names are carried with their material in this volume, others contributed significantly to the final product. These persons served as facilitators of discussion and contributed to the refinement of ideas:

Bill Bruster, Central Baptist Church Bearden, Knoxville, Tennessee;

Harold Bryson, New Orleans Baptist Theological Seminary, New Orleans, Louisiana;

James Carter, University Baptist Church, Fort Worth, Texas;

T. T. Crabtree, First Baptist Church, Springfield, Missouri;

Welton Gaddy, Broadway Baptist Church, Fort Worth, Texas;

Estill Jones, Georgia Baptist Convention, Atlanta, Georgia;

Ralph Langley, First Baptist Church, Huntsville, Alabama;

Roger Lovette, First Baptist Church, Clemson, South Carolina;

Fred Moffatt, Heritage Baptist Church, Annapolis, Maryland;

Doug Watterson, First Baptist Church, Knoxville, Tennessee.

Participants from the Baptist Sunday School Board of Nashville, Tennessee were: Gary Cook, Joe Stacker, Benton Williams, and James Hightower. James Barry of the Sunday School Board served as project coordinator and compiler of the material.

(Editor's Note: The reader will recognize a diversity of styles in the papers and sermons in this volume—for example, the way divisions are indicated and the use of underlining. As much as possible, we have preserved the unique styles of the various contributors to demonstrate that there are many approaches to sermon preparation and presentation.)

1
Preaching to the Contemporary Mind
C. David Matthews

You will probably agree that I have been given one of the more interesting subjects, Preaching to the Contemporary Mind. I was pleased to be given the assignment and did not wait long before beginning to look eagerly for a "contemporary mind." I perused my own congregation. None there. I looked at the congregations some of you work with. None there either. I even looked among the Methodists and Episcopalians. We have thriving churches in Greenville that are just coming out of the nineteenth century. I became very discouraged. We need this paper about like we need one on preaching to Eskimos. Finally, however, I accepted the possibility that someday one of us might actually <u>find</u> a contemporary mind and, equally unlikely, that we might have the opportunity of preaching to it. Should this improbable situation ever arise, I trust this paper will have made some contribution to our stewardship of it.

Seriously, the problem is not so much finding a contemporary mind as defining what one is. Fifteen years ago the phrase "the contemporary mind" would have been a synonym for secularism, and understanding secularism, or secularity or whatever preferred term, was the key to everything truly contemporary. In the sixties, many of us prepared for ministries that would of necessity rest heavily on apologetics. We would be defenders of the faith in a godless, secular world. We would make the gospel relevant to unbelieving congregations. Six months after I went to a university church where I could begin doing all this, the Jesus movement came to town. On its happy heels came a flood tide of every imaginable religious feeling and phenomenon. By Thanksgiving I was the

15

nearest thing to a secular person in the entire city.

This paper offers four rather obvious characteristics of our common cultural mentality and general suggestions of what challenges these characteristics offer preaching and the preacher. Now, this paper is humble . . . and proud of it. There is nothing exhaustive either about the list of characteristics or the proposed challenge they represent. Also, as an additional stab at humility, this paper may be found to be both good and original—only, the good parts are not original and the original parts are not good.

1. The Contemporary Mind Is Both Secular and Religious.

The secularity of the contemporary mind is solid but subtle, not always obvious or easily recognizable. The religiousness of the contemporary mind, while more overt, tends toward great naiveté. This means that essentially secular values, while largely hidden, run deep, like all good roots. At more superficial levels, there is much religious susceptibility and an eagerness to hear authoritative or authoritarian voices.

This poses a fundamental challenge to preaching to be "in the world" but not "of the world." This means that the preacher must know both the world and the gospel, the newspaper and the Bible. Karl Barth gave us the image of the preacher standing before the congregation with the Bible in one hand and that day's newspaper in the other.

These, then, are the two hands of preaching: relevance (represented by the hand holding the newspaper) and faithfulness (represented by the hand holding the Bible). Preaching does its work between the two poles of the eternal Word and the contemporary situation; therefore, preaching is never free from the inseparable challenges to faithfulness and to relevance. As H. Richard Niebuhr said of Christ and culture: "the relation of these two constitutes the problem." Keeping relevance and faithfulness in proper relation and balance largely constitutes the problem of preaching.

If we take the incarnational model seriously in preaching, it might well be argued that this distinction between relevance and faithfulness is a false one, at least where preaching is really preaching. True preaching, one might contend, involves both by definition. In other words, preaching can only be relevant when it is genuinely faithful to the eternal Word of God; and, conversely, faithfulness to that eternal Word which becomes flesh and dwells among us, genuine faithfulness to it, will always mean relevance. If you wish to make that point, it is a point well taken.

Since they are two different concepts, however, let us consider them separately a moment:

Relevance. Relevance is not simply the act of saying something contemporary or topical. Colin Morris says, "There is a strange idea abroad that Christianity has something to say about everything." He thinks one of the curses of our time is what he calls "conjunctional Christianity." "It betrays itself," he says, "in the titles of a thousand books and the themes of numberless conferences . . . 'Christianity and . . .'—Christianity and Communism, Christianity and Economic Problems, Christianity and Racism, Christianity and Vegetarianism, Christianity and the Challenge of the Cleckheaton Clogdancers."[1]

Relevant preaching starts not in a contemporary issue but in the historical gospel given in terms the congregation can understand. It is coming into the congregation's range with the truth of God in Christ. It is speaking the gospel to their understanding, so they can respond, "O, I see!"

We must be clear about the difference between relevance and topicality. Topicality is speaking about something current, contemporary. Relevance is speaking to me! When someone says, "That really spoke to me," whatever it was was relevant. Just because you talk about world hunger or drug abuse does not automatically make your preaching relevant.

Not only is relevance not topicality but it is also not preaching to people's desires. It is not merely popular preaching. Just because somebody liked it does not necessarily mean it was relevant preaching. Listen to one man's statement about his pastor:

> I cannot stand to hear him preach, he tortures me so. It is as though
> he looks through a window in my heart and knows exactly what I am
> like, exactly what I feel, exactly what I am thinking. He senses

feelings in me I have not even realized I felt, so that they strike me
with the force of sudden recognition. I cannot stand it. But neither
can I stand not to hear him. When I miss a week, as I sometimes
must, I feel as if some unbearable heaviness, like a fog or a mist, had
settled on me for the week.[2]

That pastor's preaching is relevant.

Now, if there is to be relevance, a preacher must certainly know
his or her people and something of what is going on in their world.
The preacher must live in that world. That, of course, will not be
enough. The preacher must know the people and care about them.
So it is a serious question how much, if at all, relevant preaching can
be separated from administration, counseling, and other forms of
pastoral work.

Faithfulness. Faithfulness to the Word of God is not preaching
that is full of biblical references and quotations. Neither is it
preaching that makes a fetish of the Bible, praising it, promoting it,
pounding it.

The question of what constitutes faithfulness to the Word of God
amounts to the old question: what is biblical preaching? For
extended help here see Leander Keck's The Bible in the Pulpit. For
our less extended purposes, let us say that biblical preaching is
interpreting and proclaiming the content or truth of the Bible. It is
interpreting and proclaiming the word of God as it comes to us
through the Bible. If this were not true, if the word of God and the
Bible were absolutely and at every point synonymous, then biblical
preaching should be nothing more than a verbatim quoting of the
Bible.

Unfortunately for most of us, it isn't that easy. Preachers must be
disciplined and creative students of the Bible. This is the one
foundational and indispensable source for all our preaching; and
letting it be that, consciously making it that, is what faithfulness to
the Word of God means.

The problem with many shortcuts in preaching, such as preaching
another person's sermon, is that they represent at least mild acts of
unfaithfulness to the Word of God. In preaching, the word of God

comes to my congregation not only through Christ and not only through the Bible but also through my life as the preacher—my mind, my heart, my personality. One should speak what one has heard, and even when I am offering my congregation what amounts to the "hearing" of someone else, it should be only after that truth has become for me a genuine "hearing." Otherwise, I am short-circuiting the process and something of the dynamic of preaching is lost.

2. The Contemporary Mind Is Striving for Simplicity.

This characteristic seems about as self-evident as any that could be mentioned. The contemporary mind is not keen on either ambiguity or uncertainty; thus, we witness the popularity of endless forms of fundamentalism. Whether this striving for simplicity is due to anxiety or lethargy is not always easy to say.

As a result of this striving, the people in our congregations are courted by an endless number of hucksters and some honest people with a simple answer for every kind of complex problem. They are everywhere, simple answers for marital problems, parenting problems, psychological problems, faith problems. They are mostly long on promise and short on delivery.

This characteristic of the contemporary mind presents for preaching a challenge to clarity. It is easier sought than achieved.

Gardiner Taylor has given the best answer I have heard to the question of how many points a sermon should have. "At least one," he said. You probably learned, though you may have forgotten, that every sermon should have one central idea, one message expressible in a single sentence that states "what the sermon is about."

Most of us need to simplify our preaching in much the same way we need to simplify our life-styles. Not through oversimplification and the irresponsible habits of mind and heart that produce it, but through a disciplined simplification. Who was it who said the Incarnation is "an exercise in cosmic simplification"? And in the Incarnation is our best model. A disciplined simplification means a focusing, a purifying, a clearer vision of what matters and what is extraneous. This simplification will not make the preaching task easier but more difficult. Alfred North Whitehead, in his book on the philosophy of nature, said in natural philosophy one should always seek simplicity and distrust it. So, in preaching.

Now it is certain to be granted that good preaching deals with mysteries that do not lend themselves to mathematical precision. But the problem with most of our unclear preaching is not that our hearers are overwhelmed with a sense of mystery by our profound speech. They are "underwhelmed" by our vague and random use of words and concepts with a sense of confusion—or worse, apathy. The only response that is worse than "What is he talking about?" is "Who cares what he is talking about?"

In this day of striving for simplicity, preaching must strive after clarity, making understanding a major goal. "After all," writes Clyde Fant, "we are speaking to people, not about subjects."[3]

3. The Contemporary Mind Is Distrusting of Words.

Let's blame the advertising industry. It is an easy mark. American advertising has ingenuously perfected the subtle use of language to seduce. So much so that the average person feels that he or she has been "had" too often. But not just advertising, think of all the Watergate phenomenon represents at this point.

Unfortunately, too, we who must deal with this problem have helped create it. Samuel Butler spoke once of the "irritating habit of theologians and preachers of telling little lies in the interest of a great truth." Ministerial exaggeration is almost taken for granted in some quarters. Beyond the multitude of jokes about it, Elizabeth Achtemeier suggests more serious exaggerations we make in the interest of the truth of God: we exaggerate the "immorality of groups we do not like," we exaggerate "simplistic differentiations between Christian and non-Christian living," we exaggerate "how easy it is to live out the gospel," we exaggerate "how effortlessly life's difficulties can be overcome."

Lies do not ultimately serve truth. They make truth harder to see or trust. What an enormous indictment on the pulpit today that it finds itself with something of a credibility problem.

This distrusting of words in the contemporary mind presents

preaching with a challenge to honesty. This honesty in the use of words, however, must draw from a deeper honesty in the person of the preacher. A word may be important about what this honesty does and does not mean.

History is replete with illustrations of our propensity for making gods out of good ideas. In our recent cultural history, we have carried the concept of personal integrity to an extreme and twisted it into a perversion. For a while it would not have been surprising if "I Gotta Be Me" had become our national anthem. We all know countless colleagues for whom "honesty" became a ticket out of the ministry. Their concerns to be "persons of integrity" so diminished their willingness to identify and accommodate that their sphere of ministry was reduced to disappearance. There is hardly a more delicate or important balance than that between pastoral identification (the capacity and willingness to meet people where they are) and personal integrity (the capacity for saying both yes and no and the unwillingness to respond to just any and every call).

The preacher needs to cultivate a ruthless honesty in his or her developing self-understanding, but the preacher must remember that personhood grows not only out of holding oneself in fidelity to one's convictions but also out of giving oneself away in caring relationships. There is an integrity possible, surely, that equips one, in the words of Paul, to speak the truth in love (see Eph. 4:15).

4. The Contemporary Mind Is Accustomed to Quality Media of Communication.

The contemporary mind is a bombarded mind, routinely exposed to all manner and media of communication. The quality and worth of what is communicated may be seriously questioned, but the quality and sophistication of the methods of communication cannot.

Also, this is a generation "accustomed to acting primarily on visual stimuli," according to Elizabeth Achtemeier.

> The picture on the billboard, the image on the television screen, the visual effects of the newest movie—these are the symbols that capture modern imagination. Color, light, action, but also texture and scent, taste and speed—these form the ambience of our life. We live

and move and have our being in a world of soft fabrics and eye-
catching colors, of fizzing drinks and dizzying rides, of flashing signs
and perfumed aromas—in short, in a world which seeks to stimulate
every one of our senses . . . the preacher must, therefore, translate
the biblical message into one that awakens all the senses, into words
that cause a congregation (in addition to hearing) also to see and feel
and smell and taste.[4]

This bombarded contemporary mind is, therefore, discriminat-
ing. People practice a largely unconscious selectivity—tuning in,
tuning out. Generalities, inflated language, irrelevant ideas, and
other staples of much modern preaching are ever so easy to tune
out.

Fred Craddock has a little anecdote about a layman who com-
plained to his pastor that he was just not being addressed by his
sermons. The pastor dismissed the complaint and admonished the
layman not to be so small-minded and provincial. Sometime later,
the two were attending a church convention together in another
city. When the pastor showed some anxiety about the possibility
that they would get lost in this vast metropolis, the layman assured
him that there was no reason to fear. And with that, he produced
from the rear seat of the car a globe of the world.

How instructive it would be for us if everyone would quit lying to
us about our preaching. What are they really hearing? Theron Price
was telling me once of having to listen to a certain ill-prepared
preacher. He observed, "The only way he could have said less would
have been to have talked longer." ☺

The strange sophisticiation of the contemporary mind with regard
to communication methods and media, if not to content, presents for
preaching a challenge to creativity. Creativity is not the opposite of
the simplicity we discussed earlier; in fact, they require each other.
Neither is creativity mere embellishment or the use of some
homiletical "special effects." Somerset Maugham once said of certain
writers: "Their flash effects distract the mind They destroy their
persuasiveness; you would not believe a man was very intent on
ploughing a furrow if he carried a hoop with him and jumped
through it at every other step."[5]

Creativity will mean the enrichment of every step in the preaching process. It will mean the recovery of a sense of craftsmanship, almost lost not only in preaching but everywhere. It will not require cleverness so much as commitment. Where the idea developed that creativity is a substitute for perseverence one might well ponder since truly creative people, whatever the field, are invariably disciplined in their craft.

I want to make a case for an unpopular and almost completely forsaken practice. I am hesitant about even bringing it up. I would as soon suggest to modern homemakers that they forsake the electric range and the microwave oven to resume the ancestral practice of cooking on a wood burning stove, with the attendant cutting and chopping and hauling and lighting that today are engaged in only as an ironic luxury by people affluent enough to own fireplaces. My suggestion has about as much chance catching on in an age of instant everything as a covered wagon. Still, at whatever risks, I want to advocate the discipline of writing, of manuscript preparation, in preaching.

What I mean is not the preparation of a formal manuscript, with so many characters per line, lines per page, and so forth, as if every sermon were going to the published on Monday morning. What I mean is the kind of preparation that produces on paper somewhere, in some form, the words one intends to utter in the pulpit: all of them. Not an expanded outline, which is appropriate to only one stage in the process, and then only sometimes, but every word.

I believe I know at least most of the arguments against this approach. For the most part, they amount to arguments against the public <u>reading</u> or the memorization of sermons, neither of which I am advocating. I know it is said that a manuscript inhibits or confuses the preacher or that it creates a "paper barrier" between the preacher and the congregation. But such problems result from the misuse of a manuscript rather than the use of one. Also, such criticisms usually have in mind a formal manuscript, which <u>is</u> most difficult to use in the pulpit, and assume that the manuscript will be carried into the pulpit, while it may not be.

Certainly preaching is an oral medium, not a printed one, but that hardly disqualifies a written preparation. Consider how many writers in the worlds of the media, the theater, and politics write exclusively for speaking. When it is being done by so many others, why is it unthinkable that the preacher can learn to write for speaking?

I checked this out with our own local television station in Greenville: every word that is spoken on the air is in some written form first, with few exceptions such as interview responses and talk shows which usually have the safeguard of being videotaped. In network programming and commercials, of course, precise wording and timing are even more meticulously attended.

In such a world of economized language and sophisticated techniques in communication, the even partially extemporaneous preacher is either profoundly gifted or foolish. If we don't think we need the discipline of writing, let us explain why the Scherers and the Buttricks and most of the others people have really listened to (including Billy Graham, as far as I can tell) have thought they did.

Conclusion

Finally, however the contemporary mind may be characterized, vis-à-vis the minds of other times and places, something remains the same: the human mind was created by God and for God, and it knows its Master's voice. That voice has been heard most distinctly in an old, old story, not in what is merely new. Much preaching may not be reaching the contemporary mind because it has not reached back far enough.

When I was a preschooler, my parents and I would frequently drive from our home in Tyler, Texas, thirty miles out in the country to the farm where my dad was raised and where some of my relatives still live. That was a very happy place for me; and among the many vivid recollections I have of the farm, some have to do with that thirty-mile car ride. We drove by a dairy, acres of roses growing in fields of sand, and a lake.

The little oil field town of Van is only a few miles from the farm. When we had driven through Van, we would come to a fork in the road. My dad would ask, "Dave, do you want to go the old road or the new road?"

The old road was the original way from the farm into Van and was still a dirt road. My dad had traveled that road, on horses and wagons and in trucks and cars, all his life. The new road was a smooth, paved highway. It was longer but faster, and it was also less interesting. I always chose the old road. It pleased my dad, of course. Usually as he turned down the dirt road he would break into a line or two of an old hymn that I never heard anywhere else until a few years ago. He made it fit our situation so well that it was literally years before I realized its true meaning. "The old road is the only road that leads home to God."

What is most truly new, what is most genuinely contemporary, contains within it what is most old. The Word of God sent, the Word we preach, is ancient and new because it is eternal.

Notes

1. Colin Morris, *The Word and the Words* (Nashville: Abingdon Press, 1975), p. 57.

2. John Killinger, *The Centrality of Preaching in the Total Task of the Ministry* (Waco: Word Books, 1969), p. 21.

3. Clyde Fant, *Preaching for Today* (New York: Harper & Row Publishers, 1975), p. 139.

4. Elizabeth Achtemeier, *Creative Preaching* (Nashville: Abingdon Press, 1980), p. 14.

5. Somerset Maugham, *Summing Up* (New York: Arno Press, 1938), p. 43.

On Being Humble
1 Peter 5:1-11

There is so much about humility in the Bible that there ought to be more of it in the pulpit. I know what you are thinking: there ought to be more of it in the pulpit in more ways than one! Of course, you are right. A sermon on humility does not guarantee that there is actually any humility in the pulpit.

Allow me a personal word before we proceed. I recognize that there are some sermons I am not qualified to preach. That doesn't always stop me, but sometimes it does. I have never, for example, preached a sermon on astrophysics. I have never preached on how to work a Rubiks cube or play subpar golf. I cannot preach on being the perfect husband or the perfect parent or the perfect pastor. The list is pretty long.

Of course, I am an expert on humility. I've waited all these years to tell you how humble I am. I take great pride in my humility and frequently thank God that I am not as other people. Everywhere I go I can almost hear people saying, "Isn't he humble and lovable!" If you are believing all of this, I have some oceanfront property in the panhandle of Texas I'd like to sell you.

No, humility is not my best thing, and I am humble enough to say so. As Howard Cosell says, "We've got to tell it like it is."

If that's so, why am I preaching this sermon on humility? Because the people who were willing to do it for me weren't qualified either, and the two or three who were qualified wouldn't do it to save their lives. That's humility for you.

Of course, there is the distinct possibility that you are not even interested in the subject of humility. That would not make you different from most people. As a culture we don't exactly specialize in humility. We specialize in Super Bowls, movies called "10" (the symbol of physical perfection), and books like *Real Men Don't Eat Quiche*. "Real men don't take guff from French maitre d's." "Real men don't itemize their tax deductions." And real men don't think much of concepts like humility.

The fifth chapter of 1 Peter is full of practical exhortations and personal words that have mainly to do with how these first-century Christians were to relate. A key concept in all of this is humility. It is about other things, but they all more or less relate to the spirit of humility.

There is a lot of confusion about what humility is, at least the kind the New Testament calls for. This is so much so that a lot of people who are genuinely humble, in the highest and best sense of the word, don't know it. And a lot of people who think they are humble, maybe all who think they are, are not. I think it's a good question whether it ever occurs to genuinely humble people that they are humble.

Humble, as you know, can refer to a person's actual, physical situation in the world, or it can refer to a person's attitude, quite apart from external circumstances. A person's station in life may be humble, usually meaning that the person is poor and without influence; or a person may be of humble origins, which also has to do with social or economic status.

In the Old Testament, the concept of humility is almost exclusively related to people who are in affliction, poverty, and suffering. Go all the way back to the beginning of Israel's history and you can understand something of why. The Israelites were acutely aware of their lowly status as slaves in Egypt; and because God delivered them from their afflictions, they could never regard him as the upholder of a social system built on pride and wealth. God is the one who delivers the humble, but brings down the haughty.

When to be humble means to be poor and afflicted, there is often a willingness to acknowledge one's helplessness and dependence. It is not always the case. Sometimes the poor and afflicted can be as arrogant and self-centered as any wealthy person. But the point is, in the Old Testament, humility had to do primarily with social/

political/economic status in the world, and God was generally seen as being on the side of the humble.

In the New Testament, humility refers more to subjective character traits than to external situations of affliction or poverty. Here humility becomes a Christian virtue, a way of living in the Spirit. Practically stated, humility means a lack of concern for one's own prestige and a valuing of others above oneself.

There is so much emphasis on humility in the New Testament that we must conclude it was regarded as a most important trait in the life of the early church. In 1 Peter, for example, the recipients of the letter were already humble in the first sense. They were of lowly status in the world. They were without power and influence. Now they were being encouraged in a different humility, one that had to do with their relationships in the church and to God himself.

(Read 1 Pet 5:1-5.)

We do not know whether these "elders" were official church leaders or simply venerated older people in the church, but they obviously gave leadership. The point is that they were not to be domineering or bossy, but were to tend "the flock" as "examples" of the "chief Shepherd" (vv. 3-4). The younger were to be subject to the elders, and <u>all</u> were to be clothed "with humility toward one another" (v. 5).

Now, please notice this, humility is called for in the church, not just because it is a good thing in and of itself, like "being sweet." It is called for because it is <u>the only way people can live together as Christians</u>.

Humility is not an individual and isolated form of piety. It is not even primarily an attitude toward or about yourself. We have always thought it was. Therefore, you know whom we have regarded as humble? The self-pitying person, the person who is negative on himself or herself, often the depressed person. I am convinced that a lot of what we have called humility has been psychological and spiritual sickness. In fact, a lot of downright egomania disguises itself as what we call humility.

Listen to the words of the so-called humble person: "Poor me," he says, "I can't do anything right"; "I don't belong in such company,"

she says, "I'd just be in the way"; "I'm sorry to take up your time,"
he says, "because I know you have so many more important things to
do"; "I wish there was something I could do in the church," she says,
"but I just don't have any talents." You've heard all of that, right?
These are people for whom all of life is an apology, people who
should have been throw rugs or door mats. These people are so busy
putting themselves down that they can't even look you in the eye.
They are people who, when we sing "At the Cross," still like to sing
"for such a worm as I."

That isn't humility, and such people are miles from what the New
Testament is calling for. Listen to their language. They are not
humble. They are caught in a reverse kind of pride. They are so
preoccupied with themselves that they are driving everybody they
know crazy.

Let me give you something on this from William Temple:

> Humility does not mean thinking less of yourself than of other
> people, nor does it mean having a low opinion of your own gifts. It
> means freedom from thinking about yourself one way or the other at
> all. . . . The humility which consists in being a great deal occupied
> about yourself, and saying you are of little worth, is not Christian
> humility. It is one form of self-occupation and a very poor and futile
> one at that.[1]

Humility is not so much how Christians are to feel about themselves, as it is how they are to relate to each other.

You see, those early churches which received the epistle we call
1 Peter were made up of some of the same stuff as churches today:
immaturity, insecurity, the need for attention, the need to boss, the
need to dominate.

So, they were easily offended, made mountains out of mole hills,
took sides, insisted on their own rights, got into little power
struggles, and generally produced fractures in the body of Christ.
They had to be reminded that humility was to characterize their
relationships to each other. They were to love one another, "in
honour preferring one another" if they were to live together as the
church of Jesus Christ (Rom. 12:10).

Humility, as a relational concept, simply meant putting the other first. It also meant putting God first, letting God be God.

(Read 1 Pet. 5:5-8.)

As surely as humility is an expression of love in our relationships to each other, it is an expression of faith in our relationship to God. Faith is not just believing in God, but letting him be Lord. The extent to which a person lets God be Lord, genuinely acknowledges the lordship of God, is the extent to which that person is humble.

Charles Haddon Spurgeon once said, "Humility is to make the right estimate of one's self." The right estimate of yourself is not to see yourself as a worm, but to see that you are not God. Because God is the Lord, therefore, the pressure is off me to fill that role; and because by his grace I am accepted as I am, the pressure is off me to prove I have value and worth. I am not God, but I am not a worm. I am God's child. Humility is making the right estimate of oneself.

So, do you want to be humble? Maybe you want it more than you realize. I think most of us would secretly like to let our arrogance and pride go. We just don't know we can.

You can't become humble by getting a grip on yourself, gritting your teeth, and repeating: "I will be humble. I will be humble." You follow the light of the Lord's leading—you let him be Lord—and that kind of faith produces, as a kind of by-product, true humility.

Like so many of those first-century Christians, too often we simply give lip service to this lordship while, in fact, we are still following all the wrong lights—as in the former days of our ignorance.

I learned something about sea turtles recently. Maybe you have seen the great loggerheads or the green turtles. These impressive creatures come out of the water at night to lay their eggs in the sand of the shore. When hatching time comes, the baby turtles hatch at night and in the very early morning. They are attracted to certain kinds of light, and ordinarily follow sunlight reflected on the ocean and head for the water.

A young man named Jim Hoover, who lives on Miami Beach, discovered that they have a very special problem there. Miami Beach, of course, is a solid row of lights from hotels, condominiums, swimming pools, parking lots, and so forth. And for the baby turtles these lights are on the wrong side of the shore. They beckon these newborn creatures like "glowing fingers of death."

So you can see baby turtles "crushed by the hundreds on crowded Collins Avenue, or baked in the summer heat at the foot of parking meters." You can see them "just after sunup, desperately trying to climb the seawalls in back of the beach, scrambling over one another in a frantic, primal drive to reach the light—the wrong light, in the wrong direction."[2]

This is something of what the writer of 1 Peter knew must not happen to the first Christians, the new Christians of the first century. Despite all the pressures that are on them, despite the attraction of the wrong ways—especially when they have been weakened by suffering—they must be "firm in [their] faith" (v. 9, RSV). Central to this faith is the spirit of humility, the spirit of Christ, in which there is so much light, and life, and promise.

(Read 1 Pet. 5:10-11.)

Notes

1. William Temple, *Christ in His Church* (London: Macmillan Co., 1925).
2. Cliff Yudell, "Turtle Patrol," *Eastern Review*, February, 1983 (reprinted from *GEO Magazine*). Copyright 1982, Knapp Communications Corp.

2
Preaching and Church Growth
Calvin Miller

The Book of Jonah is the story of a reluctant preacher. Jonah's message as we have come to know it is: "Yet forty days, and Nineveh shall be overthrown" (Jonah 3:4).

The message is a brief eight words. Surely there is more: some clever and imaginative introduction written in the lost oral manuscript. There must have been iterations, poetry, and exegesis. But they are gone, and those eight words are all we know of the lost sermon. Such a miniature message seems anticlimactic. Even the king of Nineveh had more to say than Jonah (Jonah 3:7-9). But the lost sermon was preached and bore a stern word of necessity.

Jonah 3:10 states the point of the lost sermon: "And God saw their works, that they turned from their evil way; and God repented of the evil, that he had said that he would do unto them; and he did it not." The results of sermons in the Bible seem generally to be stated and of great importance. This is true of both Testaments. Acts 2:40-41 speaks of the dramatic results of Peter's Pentecostal sermon: "Howbeit many of them which heard the word believed; and the number of the men was about five thousand" (Acts 4:4). While Jonah omitted the statistics of his sermon, Luke carefully noted Simon's. Preaching in the New Testament seems to closely emulate the authoritative style of the prophets in the Old Testament. Ever cloaked in other worldly authority, preaching became the vehicle that the early church rode into the arena of evangelizing the Roman Empire. As common people of Galilee once marveled at the authority of Christ in the Sermon on the Mount (Matt. 7:28-29), so the authority of Scripture-based sermons became the defense—sometimes the sole

32

defense—of the men and women who pressed the strong alternatives of the good news.

The texts of these sermons are included in only a few cases and are almost absent from the accounts of the apostles. From John the Baptist to the end of the New Testament era the sermon, like the church itself, flamed with apocalyptic zeal. The prophets had preached strong declarations of the direction of God in history in the sermons of rabbis and prophets. These messengers, like those of the New Testament, thundered their strong "heaven or hell" demands to their hearers.

Following Pentecost, the sermon was possessed of a new spiritual union, where the preacher and the Holy Spirit were joined in a powerful alliance. The sermon was inspired by the Spirit. Because of his direct alliance with the Trinity, the preacher had the right to speak with God's authority, demanding immediate action and visible decisions. This "right-now" ethic saw the sermon in terms of the demand of God. When God demanded decisions, they could be tabulated as soon as the sermon was finished. Sheep could immediately be divided from goats. Those on God's side could be counted as well as those who were not.

The specific message was delivered by him who possessed the call—the charisma. The rules of the primitive homiletics were not defined. The sermon was the man: the medium, the message. The product was instant and visible. Faith could be tabulated by those who cried in the streets that they believed or those who admitted to baptism or those who showed up for the breaking of bread and prayers.

Following the first "head counts" of those who were baptized— the fire of evangelism spread, pushed on by the hot winds of Greek and Aramaic sermons. Congregations sprang up in celebration of the sermons that called them into being. Without institutional structure or programs or buildings, the church celebrated the simple center of her noncomplex worship—the sermon and that which the sermon created: the company of the committed, the fellowship of believers.

The sermon was not celebrated as art, though doubtless art may have been an aspect of delivery. Art was not so important in the panicky apocalypticism of century one. Zeal raged in the bright light of Pentecost, not art. The sermon was the means of reaching the last, desperate age of humanity. One needed not to polish phrases or study word roots—the kingdom was at hand—there wasn't time to break ground for a seminary. Church administration went begging. On the eve of Armageddon, committees and bureaus were unimportant. There was only one point to be made. All human wisdom was one set of alternatives: repent or perish.

To come full circle, where we began, this was also Jonah's sermon: repent or perish. Jonah's sermon, like those of the New Testament era, was not a notable document. The sermon was the workhorse of urgent evangelism.

Jonah's sermon was powerful simply because it was not ornate. He who cries fire in a theater does not need to be an orator. Indeed, the man who cries fire has a message of such priority that it is allowed to interrupt the art of actors. It is not an offense to the years of discipline to set aside the drama for the urgent and unadorned word which has come. "The theater is on fire!" The bearer of the word bears it with burden and rates his effectiveness on how fast the theater is cleared, not on the ovation of the desperate. The alarmist is not out for encores but empty seats. His business is rescue.

The Book of Jonah concerns such reluctant and apocalyptic preaching.

Jonah's story makes it clear that it was a necessity for Jonah to speak. The royal family sitting at last in the ashes of national repentance illustrates how effective his urgency was.

Without encore, Jonah delivered the word. He cried fire, and Nineveh heard and believed his alarm. This zealous declaration is the word of God as it is preached in growing churches. Those who would speak an artistic word must do it in churches already built. Only those who cry fire can serve in the evangelical ghettos of the unredeemed and make it work.

Further, those who admire the Fosdicks and Maclarens—and they are to be admired—must see that the artistry of their sermons would be passed by in the slums of London where Booth's drums and horns sounded not a "trumpet voluntary" to call men to the queen's chapel but the "Oom-pah-pah" of the Cross. "Are you washed in the blood of the Lamb?" was such an urgent question that it nauseated Anglicans even as it intrigued the poor and downtrodden of England with its zealous demands.

What did Booth say? Who knows? Who cares?

What did Whitefield say? What Sunday?

What Finney, what Wesley, what Mordecai Hamm? To be sure, some of their sermons survive them. But essentially they viewed their sermons not in the Chrysostom tradition but the tradition of the Baptizer of Christ: "O generation of vipers, who hath warned you to flee from the wrath to come? Bring forth fruits worthy of repentance" (Luke 3:7-8). Or Simon Peter cried: "Save yourselves from this untoward generation" (Acts 2:40).

Here and there men like Jonathan Edwards combined the best of literary tradition and apocalyptic zeal. But there was a real sense in which the Mathers, the Edwards, and the other Puritans supplied a presoap-opera generation with a cultural center. The better their apocalypse, the higher the other world fever of their gospel contagion. Their fiery tirades began to resemble the spirit of a matador, and the amens were the enthusiastic olés, where the champion was not Jehovah but the preacher. Kate Caffrey writes:

A strong style was favored—in 1642 John Cotton recommended preaching after the manner of Christ, who, he said, "let fly poynt blanck"—and the hearers judged each performance like professional drama critics. Two sermons on Sunday and a lecture-sermon or weeknight meeting, usually on Thursday, were the custom, with fines of up to five shillings for absence from church. Only those who wished need go to the weeknight sermon, which was accompanied by no prayers or other teaching. Yet they were so popular in the sixteen-thirties that the General Court of Massachusetts tried to make every community hold them on the same day, to cut down all the running about from one town to the next. The preachers protested that it was in order to hear sermons that people had come to New England, so the court contented itself with the mild recommendation that listeners should at least be able to get home before dark.

Even condemned criminals joined in the vogue for sermons. On March 11, 1686, when James Morgan was executed in Boston, three sermons were preached to him by Cotton and Increase Mather and Joshua Moody (so many came to hear Moody that their combined weight cracked the church gallery), and the prisoner delivered from the scaffold a stern warning to all present to take heed from his dread example.

Sermons were so important that it is impossible to overestimate them. Hourglasses, set up by the minister, showed the sermons' length: a bare hour was not good enough. People brought paper and inkhorns to take copious notes in a specially invented shorthand; many thick notebooks filled with closely written sermon summaries have been preserved. The meetinghouse rustled with the turning of pages and scratching of pens. Sermons were as pervasive then as political news today; they were read and discussed more eagerly than newspapers are now.[1]

These intellectualized, zealous Massachusetts Bay sermons were celebrated by sermon lovers throughout New England. In these meetinghouses the sermon grew in new performance value. And yet the zeal and urgency were viewed as part of the performance. The tendency remains. Now the zealot is a performer, and the sermon a monologue celebrated for its emotional and statistical success. The growing church still focuses on the sermon as a cultural agreement as well. The burden is at once urgent and entertaining. The preacher feels the burden of his word as the "fire crier" feels the pain of his office. But he feels also the pleasure of its success which is his reputation.

Ego being the force it is, the urgency of the cry often becomes a secondary theme. A preacher's artistry may eclipse his zeal.

Herman Melville told of Father Mapple's sermon on the Book of Jonah in *Moby Dick*. Remembering that Jonah's sermon is not recorded at all in the Bible, listen to Mapple's artistic recounting of the brief eight words of Jonah 3:4:

Then God spake unto the fish; and from the shuddering cold and blackness of the sea, the whale came breeching up towards the warm and pleasant sun, and all the delights of air and earth; and 'vomited out Jonah upon the dry land'; when the word of the Lord came a second time; and Jonah, bruised and beaten—his ears, like two seashells, still multitudinously murmuring of the ocean—Jonah did the Almighty's bidding. And what was that, shipmates? To preach the truth to the face of Falsehood! That was it!

This, shipmates, this is that other lesson; and woe to that pilot of the living God who slights it. Woe to him whom this world charms from Gospel duty! Woe to him who seeks to pour oil upon the waters when God has brewed them into a gale! Woe to him who seeks to please rather than to appal! Woe to him whose good name is more to him that goodness! Woe to him who, in this world, courts not dishonour! Yea, woe to him who, as the great Pilot Paul has it, while preaching to others is himself a castaway![2]

But perhaps Father Mapple's art can afford to be more obvious than his zeal: he is preaching in a church already there and is not himself delivering urgency but a sermon on urgency!

For years I have felt myself trapped in this quandary. Growing a church causes me to speak of redemption, frequently and earnestly. My sermons often sounded to me more zealous than artistic. It was their intent to draw men to Christ, in which pursuit my church was coming to be.

But you may object, "Was it only sermon that created your church? Did you not use the manuals and conventional machinery of the church and parachurch?" Yes. There were mailing programs, and such radio and newspaper ads as we could manage. Did not the sermon become second place in the issue of the church? Bill Hull in a previous symposium said:

> Let us candidly confront this chilling claim that the pulpit is no longer the prow of the church, much less of civilization, as Herman Melville visualized it in *Moby Dick*. Ask any pulpit committee after months of intensive investigation and travel: How many pastors in the Southern Baptist Convention are even trying to build their careers on the centrality of preaching? . . . Subtle but excruciating pressures are brought to bear on the minister today to spend all of the week feverishly engineering some spectacular scheme designed to draw attention to his church, then on Saturday night to dust off somebody else's clever sermon outline (semantic gimmickry) for use the next morning.[3]

Is this not so? I think to some degree it is.

But there are some of us who don't want it to be. We feel called to do the work of an evangelist and believe that urgency can have some class and be done with some artistry and/or enlightenment. For years I have listened to the sermons of Richard Jackson, pastor at North Phoenix Baptist Church, with great debt to his example. After he finished a long section in the passion passage of John, I saw the Cross in a new light. During the preaching of more than a year of sermons on the Gospel of John, more than six hundred were added to his church by baptism. Perhaps Pastor Jackson has taken the burden of urgency to the Greek New Testament and the credible commentators and did his best to say, "Here is enlightened urgency."

For those who minister to growing churches, I have seen the same struggle to maintain balance. Hordes of popular parachurch lecturers and concert artists come through town, and each in turn have members of their congregations on their huge arena of influence. Often the growing church pastor has to reckon with the doctrinal and philosophical weaknesses of various viewpoints. In this context it gets harder and harder to lead a congregation in the direction of sound evangelism and a more artistic appeal.

Along with these never ceasing pressures toward fundamental activism, the pastor must also reckon with the various theological fads that sweep the culture from decade to decade. Again Bill Hull has described our dilemma:

> Sample the marketplace for the religious wares being peddled there today: charismatic blessing, millennial visions, infallible Bibles. Measured by the attention which they receive, one would suppose that the ultimate issues facing Christianity today are whether it is legitimate and necessary to speak in tongues, whether Israel is about to trigger the end of the world, and whether some undiscovered autograph is free from scientific and historical error. I dare you to set this agenda beside the preaching of Jesus and Paul. It is like moving from the foothills into the mountains. Let us not mount the pulpit to debate peripheral questions or to speculate on esoteric curiosities. We are not put there to haunt the sideshows of life or to substitute

fanciful theories for the eternal gospel. We are there to preach Jesus Christ as Lord. . . .

With disaster staring him in the face, Churchill took up the weapon of his adversary and began to do battle with words. From a concrete bombshelter deep underground, he spoke to the people of Britain not of superiority but of sacrifice, not of conquest but of courage, not of revenge but of renewal. Slowly but surely, Winston Churchill talked England back to life. To beleaguered old men waiting on their rooftops with buckets of water for the fire bombs to land, to frightened women and children huddled behind sandbags with sirens screaming overhead, to exhausted pilots dodging tracer bullets in the midnight sky, his words not only announced a new dawn but also conveyed the strength to bring it to pass.

No wonder Ruskin described a sermon as "thirty minutes to raise the dead." That is our awesome assignment: to put into words, in such a way that our hearers will put into deeds, the new day that is ours in Jesus Christ our Lord.[4]

His argument is well stated; and it is this set of arguments which, when placed in the ecclesia of the growing church, becomes its preachment.

The preachment of the lordship of Christ is that which undergirds a kind of gross national product hermeneutics. Class, excellence, and literary accounts are laid on the altar of production and baptismal quota. This idea is not so much to preach Christ as to preach "souls down the aisle." There is no place on the annual letter to measure how well the pastor of a growing church preaches Christ, but there are many, many slots and boxes which record altar response, baptisms, and dollars given.

The competition becomes fierce. The drive to become a "top tenner" is the direct enemy of excellence in both sermons and theology. Preaching becomes epigrammatic, sloganistic, and cute. Theology shifts to shibboleths. Great stands are taken weekly from this verbal inspiration of Scripture, door-to-door evangelism, and chain-of-command family psychology.

The growing church must see the sermon as the ultimate in dialogue. I base this kind of sentence on the idea that dialogues enlighten and change lives. Martin "I-Thou" Buber makes an excellent point about the nature of truth when he says that truth is not so much "in us" as "between us." The man in the street would use a street proverb to say, "Two heads are better than one." This "Poor Richardism" is the basis of good preaching. The best sermons ever in growing churches do not strut and scream "repent or perish!" The best sermons entreat in dialogue, "Come now, and let us reason together, saith the Lord: though your sins be as scarlet, they shall be as white as snow" (Isa. 1:18).

Is there no authority then in the sermon of the growing church? Yes, but it is not a thou-shalt-not authority; it is a reasoning authority, stating that our defense of the gospel is ever to state a "reason" for the hope that is in us (1 Pet. 3:15).

Dogmatism is "authority-sclerosis." It is an incessant filibuster—never mute, always deaf! Talking is easier and much louder than thinking. The growing church too often cannot celebrate new truth, for it is too long screaming the old ones. The familiar is the creed, the unfamiliar is liberalism and dangerous revisionism. This thinking man off the street may want to ask questions and enter into dialogue, but the truth is that he finds that trying to ask a question is like shouting into the gales or trying to quote the flag salute at a rock concert. His need for reasons seems buried in the noise.

I have always been interested in Huck Finn's reasons for deciding to go with Tom Sawyer to hell rather than the fundamentalist Miss Watson to heaven:

> Then she told me all about the bad place, and I said I wished I was there. She got mad, then, but I didn't mean no harm. All I wanted was to go somewheres; all I wanted was a change, I wasn't particular. She said it was wicked to say what I said; said she wouldn't say it for the whole world; she was going to live so as to go to the good place. Well, I couldn't see no advantage in going where she was going, so I made up my mind I wouldn't try for it. But I never said so, because it would only make trouble and wouldn't do no good.
>
> Now she had got a start, and she went on and told me all about the good place. She said all a body would have to do there was to go around all day long with a harp and sing, forever and ever. So I didn't think much of it. But I never said so. I asked her if she reckoned Tom

Sawyer would go there, and, she said, not by a considerable sight. I
was glad about that, because I wanted him and me to be together.[5]

The logic of the streets is doubly plagued by such images. Why
would a robust, open-minded Christ so love an overcorseted,
dispeptic, neurotic, Scripture quoter as Miss Watson?

Each time I see a sign that says "Bible Preaching Here Every
Sunday," I am struck by the incongruity. Bible preaching has so
many press agents. Usually such signs mean only: the familiar and
expected will be rehearsed here in our characteristic way. Did
Jeremiah run an ad in the *Jerusalem World* which said in three-inch
letters on the Saturday church page: "God Said It, I Believe It, and
that Settles It." Hardly. His existentialism was so fragile, he wished
God would make him an innkeeper or quench the fire in his bones
or destroy the man who sent those birth announcements reading:
Born: a Boy, Jeremiah ben Hilkiah at Anathoth General—7 lbs. 8
ozs. of misery from his mother's womb—a lackluster crybaby who
never wrote a book entitled *Why I Preach the Pentateuch Is the
Word* and never saw his haunting *Lamentations* about his hometown
reach *Late-Great-Planet-Earth* success. But then, what can you
expect from a millennialist who had no idea who the great harlot on
the purple beast really was.

No, Bible preaching is usually not so biblical as it is a rehearsal of
a world view, friendly and familiar. Still, the preaching of the Cross,
as Paul said, is ever a kind of simplistic foolishness to those who are
perishing and a rational and wise activity to those who are being
saved. No matter what castigations we level at the typical preaching
of a typical growing church, we must admit that their preaching
seems to the populace to be an earnest understanding that Christianity is a rescue religion. To those who attend those "evangelistic"
churches, the sermon which rescues does not divert itself to play
with art or standards of excellence.

The truth is that those who boast that the real word is the word of
the scholars who understand the wide and sovereign God have less
statistical success than those who keep Jehovah on a more provincial
basis. The burning sociotheologian who cries out of world need may

be preaching to fewer and fewer each week. An understanding of the world as lost, one-dimensional, and "spiritual" is radically attractive. "The poor you have with you always" cry those who want to see the world saved now. Those who cry "Rescue the perishing" seem to have a message which attracts the masses to the gospel as a purely spiritual presupposition. There is a distrust of all that smacks of social consideration in the growing church.

J. I. Packer, a nonmainstream but very popular Anglican, writes that the modern critical movement is the beast to the Christian church which seeks to retain the power and force of evangelistic theology. The truth, says Packer, is that the critical movement has undermined real Christianity in five ways:

> First, it has undermined preaching. The true idea of preaching is that the preacher should become a mouthpiece for his text, opening it up and applying it as a word from God to his hearers, talking only in order that the text may speak itself and be heard. . . .
>
> Secondly, loss of conviction about the divine truth of the Bible has undercut teaching. Clergy are not sure what to inculcate as Christian truth; layfolk doubt whether what is taught in the Bible is worth learning. . . .
>
> Thirdly, uncertainty as to whether Bible teaching is God's truth has weakened faith.
>
> Fourthly, perplexities about Holy Scripture have discouraged lay Bible reading.
>
> Fifthly, and saddest of all, scepticism about the Bible has hidden Christ from view. We are told not to think of the person whose fourfold portrait the gospels draw, and whose many-sided mediation the epistles describe, as any more than a product of fertile religious imagination.[6]

Whether one agrees with all that Packer says, he has well captured the fears of most "evangelistic" preachers.

There is the widespread feeling that the zealous pulpit should beware those journals and publications of mainstream theology which cannot keep company with the practice.

I must confess that I myself in my years of winning people to Christ have come to see a great divorce between theology as an academic discipline and the practical bedrock of faith that is the pier of those who cry out in lonely ghettos of human need. I have often felt about Barth the way he felt about Schleiermacher. At Safenwil he needed to give his people a firmer word than would come from the permissive mainstream of the Christianity that had spanned his theology.

It is true that Gilkey in China once cried under the thumbscrews of persecution, "All my liberal presuppositions have been shattered." I can understand that. I need for myself a trustworthy word to bear the burdens of my church—a word firm enough, yet authoritarian enough to say, "Thus says the Lord—for keeps!" I need to be able to say, "God's word is a constant and undying witness to his author." Packer again identifies what the man in the street cries out for:

> Many Protestant writers today err here, accepting the witness of revelation to other truths yet sitting loose to its witness to itself. Notions such as that revelation took the form of a progress from faulty thoughts of God to more exact ones, or that it took place by divine deed and not by divine word, or that the divine inspiration of statements does not guarantee their truth, or that the scriptural record of revelation is not itself revelation, get copied from book to book without regard for the fact that they contradict revelation's own account of itself. We only truly honour the God who has spoken in His Son to us blind sinners by listening humbly, teachably, and without interrupting, to what He has to say, and by believing, on His authority, all that He is pleased to tell us—about revelation, no less than any other subject.[7]

Authority is the word in the sermon of the growing church. Still I would argue for a dialogical authority. It is not that saying "Thus saith the Lord" is wrong, and yet we are all drawn by the counsel of a friend who says, "Let us look together at what the Lord saith!" When we become more authoritarian in dialogues, then we need to be sure that when we say, "Thus Saith the Lord," we are really speaking the mind of God and not merely strong-arming our own agenda in another's more mighty name.

Finally, if we could slow the thunder a bit in favor of a slow and certain light, I think we would be a more mature people. If in our desperate dialogues over the souls of people we could find a piece of class, how happy we would be. If we could admit that Jonathan Edwards succeeded best at desperation literature, we would have found a new area of the pleasure of Christ.

The evangelistic sermon ever brags that it tells the truth, but as Sören Kierkegaard once said, "Truth is not nimble on its feet— rather it can be heavy footed and pedestrian." How can the thousands of church growing pastors be taught these gentle truths. Perhaps we need to argue for the sermon not as creation but as "procreation." What a delicious idea! God and man participating together to plan an excellence that still says <u>Jesus Saves</u> but does it with enchantment and intrigue.

This brings even the pedestrian, exegetical sermon into the realm of true creation. Not a dull repetition of sterile commentaries but rather the taste of new wine—a spell of glory—an addiction—an inebriation—a heady delirium of two meeting in an exotic fog of splendor. Well has Vladimir Nabokov said:

> Literature is invention. Fiction is fiction. To call a story a true story is an insult to both art and truth. . . . A major writer combines these three—storyteller, teacher, enchanter—but it is the enchanter in him that predominates and makes him a major writer.[8]

A major part of our problem in preaching is that people cannot really take the Bible, a literature of the past, and turn it into a reply to the present artistically. Small wonder that H. E. Fosdick criticized our antiquarian exposition by saying that the preacher was the only one who still went through life assuming that everyone was aching in curiosity to find out whatever happened to the Jebusites.

How do you make what happened to the Jebusites three thousand years ago useful? Again, it is Nabokov which answers the dilemma by saying the past needs to be dissolved in art:

> The key to the problem of reestablishing the past turns out to be the key of art. The treasure hunt comes to a happy end in a cave full of music, in a temple rich with stained glass. The gods of standard

religions are absent, or, perhaps more correctly, they are dissolved in art.[9]

Still, there is a point at which the sermon must be finished. When it is done, how shall we measure whether it has been a success? In the growing church, there must be "altar response." Yes, the last test as to its value is were there usable, spendable, countable "souls for Jesus!" And as crass as the evaluation sounds, unless the preached word encounters and changes its hearers in some way, artistry and enchantment cannot be said to have mattered much. The sermon must not at last be cute but life changing. Somerset Maugham once said of certain writers: "Their flash effects distract the mind. They destroy their persuasiveness; you would not believe a man was very intent on ploughing a furrow if he carried a hoop with him and jumped through it at every other step."[10]

When the sermon has reasoned, exhorted, pled, and pontificated; when it has glittered with art and oozed with intrigue; when it has entered into the heart of humanity and broken secular thralldom— when all of this has been done, the sermon must enter into judgment at a high tribunal. Like the person who uttered it, the sermon must hear the judgment of the last great auditor. If, indeed, every word is brought to God and the sermons of all the ages are to be listed together, one can imagine the last great gathering of the sermons of all the ages—the MARCH OF THE CASSETTES PAST THE THRONE. Every word tried from the ministry it managed—a thousand, thousand sermons—indeed, a great host which no one could number: Peter Marshall, Peter the Hermit, Peter the Apostle, Peter Piper, Peter Paul, Popes, Carl McIntire, Oral Roberts, Robert Bellarmine, John Rice, John Newton, John Hus, Prince John—a thousand, thousand words from David Brainerd to Origen, Tertullian to Swagart, Jack Van Impe to Arius all at once replying to one issue: who preached and which sermons really counted?

The God who is the friend of people and ancient lover of the sinners to whom these trillion words are addressed will cry to those sermons in his left hand—"Why did you not serve me—Why did you not love people enough to change them? You took the hearts of people, commanded their attention, but did nothing to change them. Repent ye cursed sermons to Gehenna—be burned to ashes and be scattered as nothing over chaos—for better sermons would have called chaos to unfold itself in strong creation."

Notes

1. Kate Caffrey, *The Mayflower* (New York: Stein and Day, 1974).

2. Herman Melville, *Moby-Dick; or the Whale*, (Chicago: William Benton, Publisher, 1952), pp. 35-36.

3. William E. Hull, "Called to Preach," *Search*, (1978), p. 49.

4. Ibid., p. 53.

5. Samuel Langhorne Clemens, *Adventures of Huckleberry Finn* (New York: W. W. Norton & Co., Inc., 1961-62), p. 8.

6. J. I. Packer, *God Has Spoken* (Downers Grove: InterVarsity Press, 1979), pp. 28-30.

7. Ibid., pp. 62-63.

8. Vladimir Nabokov, "How to Read, How to Write," *Esquire*, (1980), p. 64.

9. Ibid., p. 67.

10. Somerset Maugham, *Summing Up* (New York: Arno Press, 1938), p. 43.

A Worldwide Vision
Matthew 28:19-20
J. Truett Gannon

My purpose is to present Christ to you as Matthew saw him; to share with you Christ's purpose for the world as Matthew understood it; and to encourage our response to that purpose as Matthew would have wanted it.

Matthew believed that Jesus was God's great intervention in human affairs. Jesus was more than a good man. Though he was the best man who ever lived, he was the direct incarnation of his Father. Because of Christ, we are encouraged to look for God at work in the world. Through Christ, we have reason to trust the work God is doing in the world. In Christ, we can be part of that work.

As we follow Matthew's Gospel, we listen to Jesus preach the greatest sermon the world has ever heard; and we watch him live the greatest life the world has ever seen. We hear Jesus say that in him the kingdom of God has come on earth and that because of him a new covenant of grace and love has replaced the old covenant of law and legalism.

Our minds can hardly believe the response some religious leaders made to Jesus. How they perceived him as an imposter to God rather than the beloved Son of God betrays all logic.

No sense of fair play can condone how they contrived his death. They were so confused that none of their witnesses could recite their memorized accusations against Jesus with enough accuracy to enable any two of them to qualify as witnesses. Yet, they were so determined he should die that they had him put to death on the charge of the one thing he refused to be: a political messiah.

Christ died, but God resurrected him. By his power, God brought Jesus from death to life; and by his grace, God let the disciples see

47

Jesus face-to-face. Christ reaffirmed for them that he whose temple had been destroyed had indeed been raised again in three days.

A Mountaintop Commission

The gospel, however, is more than an account of a good man whom the people of his day could not keep dead, and more is involved in his resurrection appearances than just his reassuring the disciples about himself. To find that purpose, let us move with the disciples to the mountain to which Jesus had directed them.

Think of all the mountaintop experiences the disciples shared with Christ; it was from a mountaintop that Jesus preached the Sermon on the Mount. It was on a mountaintop that three of the disciples saw Jesus transfigured, and it was on a mountaintop that they heard Jesus give his greatest command and his greatest promise.

Compare this mountain encounter of Jesus and the disciples with the encounter Jesus had with Satan in the temptation experience in Matthew 4. Satan had taken Jesus to a high mountain and showed him all the kingdoms of the world. Then Satan offered to give those kingdoms to Christ if he would fall down and worship Satan.

On that mountain, Satan had offered to give the world to Christ. On the mountain, in Matthew 28, Jesus said that the kingdoms of the world have been his all along. "All authority in heaven and on earth has been given to me," he said (v. 18, RSV).

On the mountain with Satan, Jesus had said, "Begone, Satan! for it is written, 'You shall worship the Lord your God/and him only shall you serve'" (Matt. 4:10, RSV). On the last mountaintop, Jesus told his disciples to get going, too, in service to the kingdom.

After the first mountain experience, Jesus was ministered to by angels. After the last mountain experience, Jesus returned to his Father in heaven, hoping his disciples would minister unto him, too, as they obeyed his command.

We call Jesus' command to his disciples the Great Commission: "Go therefore and make disciples of all nations, baptizing them in the name of the Father and of the Son and of the Holy Spirit, teaching them to observe all that I have commanded you;" it ends with Christ's great promise, "and lo, I am with you always, to the close of the age" (v. 19). Life knows no momentum stronger than these words.

A Strategy for Winning the World

The way the early church organized itself to follow that command is an intriguing story. Jesus had left no specific plans for winning the world; he was willing to leave that to the good sense of the people who would serve him.

The first organizational strategy is seen in Acts 6. If I were to tell you the one word by which we commonly identify this episode, you would know quickly what it is about. We usually refer to it as first election of deacons. But to reduce what happened in Acts 6 to just the selection of deacons is to miss a valid point in the story.

The early church was proclaiming what God had done in Christ. As could have been expected, the response was tremendous. "The disciples were increasing in number" (Acts 6:1). What they were doing was dealing with that increase.

Growth was giving the early church problems. Individual attention was becoming more difficult to give. People were feeling neglected (Acts 6:1). Sensing that matters could only become more complex, the apostles asked for help. They were not simply electing deacons; they were reorganizing themselves to deal with the complications of growth.

Their efforts paid off. After they had found "seven men of good repute, full of the Spirit and of wisdom" (Act 6:3), the growth continued, and the people's needs were met. Acts 6:7 confirms this, "And the word of God increased; and the number of the disciples multiplied greatly."

That reorganization required a lot of adjustment. It is not easy to reshape one's life-style or one's pattern of service. Much flexibility was required by everyone.

The apostles had to become willing to let other people serve with them. They could have been jealous of their position, refusing to share responsibility for fear they would lose status if they did.

One of the trends that often happens as a church becomes large is a tendency to establish one's territory. When the church is small, every one happily shares rooms, space, and supplies. As the church becomes large, however, some share the "Hellenists' widows" fear that they will be overlooked. Some begin to resent any intrusion upon their territory. They don't want their room used by any group but theirs. Many are afraid that the larger we become, the smaller we will seem.

The apostles helped the early church meet the problems of growth by accepting those seven men as fellow disciples. They did not discourage their participation; they welcomed their service. Accepting others as fellow servants of Christ will ease our problems of growth too.

When a church grows, "old" members must be willing to let "new" members serve. It is not necessary for "old" members to step aside so that "new" members can serve; it is only required that "old" members let "new" members serve alongside. Our ministry is not lessened when we let others share it; it is strengthened.

The apostles were not being replaced, they were being helped. There could only be twelve who qualified as original disciples (Acts 1:21-22), and they had already replaced Judas. They were not replacing apostles; they were increasing them. They had twelve, but with the election of deacons there were nineteen! One of the reasons this was done so easily is because the twelve were so open and accepting of the new seven.

Some maturing was required in the seven too. It would have been so easy for them to doubt their qualifications when compared with the first twelve. Since they were not members of the original group of apostles, how could they be expected to serve alongside such great men?

When a church grows, its quality usually improves. The choir gets better as well as larger; the teachers seem better trained. Many of us do wrestle with the fear that we are not good enough to serve in so large a church which seems too great to let people like we are serve.

The seven men in Acts did not feel that way. They knew they were more than table waiters; they were fellow disciples. Though they did not qualify as apostles, they knew they were qualified to serve in some way, and they were not hesitant to do so.

Two of those seven became two of the more prominent people of the New Testament.

Stephen, "full of grace and power, did great wonders and signs among the people" (Acts 6:8). His sermon to the council is one of the best and the longest recorded in Scripture. He became the church's first martyr.

Philip went down "to a city of Samaria, and proclaimed to them the Christ" (Acts 8:5). That's more than waiting on tables! Who does not remember Philip's witness to the Ethiopian and the Ethiopian's request to be baptized? "Passing on he preached" is the way Luke closed the story about him in Acts 8:40. Philip was quite a person.

As growth comes, you will be asked to serve with people who seem much more effective than you. You must remember that like the seven, you, too, can render great service on your own.

You can also help yourself by recalling that there is no inconsequential work in the kingdom. Table waiting, like giving a cup of water in Matthew 10:42, will earn you the status of a disciple just as much as the seemingly greater deeds by those who seem superior to us. When each person uses his own gifts in serving and allows others the use of their gifts, the fellowship is enriched, the outreach is enlarged, and the spiritual maturity of every one is deepened.

A Willingness to Change

It wasn't just the twelve and the seven who had to be flexible; the widows had to adjust too. They were the ones who had been most adversely affected and the ones who would be expected to accept the most radical change.

Accustomed to being served by the apostles, they found themselves now designated to be served by substitute apostles! They could have refused. It isn't easy to be served by the associate minister when it is the pastor whom you wanted. All of us know how that feels.

The original owners of the Waffle House, Inc., are friends of mine. I knew them when there was only one franchise.

In the early days of their business, I could go by the office any afternoon, prop my feet on a desk, and spend a relaxed hour or so. When I left, one of them would even go by the storage-refrigerator and get me a few steak filets for my dinner.

As business increased, however, their afternoons became less available. I could still get the filets whenever I wanted them, but I had to get them now from an assistant. Accustomed to dealing only with the president or the treasurer, this new procedure was not easy for me.

I had to learn that my friendship with the owners would remain just as strong, the filets would continue to taste just as good, and that the new assistant was also going to become a good friend.

As I opened myself to him, our relationship deepened. Soon, our friendship was close, just as the others were. What had been just a twosome was now becoming a threesome. My willingness to change procedures did not hurt me; it gave me one of the strongest friendships I've ever known.

Every church that is effective is going to grow beyond the abilities of any one pastor to deal with every detail. Your points of contact will become fewer but your relationship will continue. Though he will not be available on a casual basis, he will remain your deep friend.

Your willingness to change procedures and be served by an associate will not hurt you, it will strengthen you. It will strengthen your church, and it will deepen your relationship with everyone.

Every Christian has to believe that God can and will work through anyone. We must be willing to risk ourselves and our ministries to the talents and integrity of others.

The early church, for example, could hardly have survived without the apostle Paul. It is likely, though, that without Ananias, the early church would not have had Paul. Can you imagine the apprehension Ananias felt as he approached the street called Straight to talk about Christ to the man who had come there to imprison people who believed in Christ? Yet he went, and because of his openness to new people, Paul was accepted by the fellowship.

The cause of missions would have been weakened without Paul. It is likely, however, that without Barnabas, the church in Antioch which started missions would never have known of Paul.

After Paul's conversion, his past opposition to the church continued to hinder him. He had been defied in Damascus (Acts 9:23) and rejected in Jerusalem (Acts 9:26). It took a lot of grace for someone to believe in a man like Paul.

Barnabas, however, was willing to trust his ministry to Paul. He and Paul met with the Antioch church for one full year, each accepting the other and the church accepting both. And it may have been just that spirit of acceptance (Acts 11:25-26) that caused the disciples to be called Christians "first in Antioch."

Growth always brings problems and asks for new procedures to meet the problems. Are we willing to change?

Someone handed me a list of differences between a live church and a dead church. I don't remember the author, but I do remember some of the contrasts:

—A live church will always have parking problems; a dead one won't.

—A live church is always going to be filled with people who find it increasingly difficult to remember every one's name. In a dead church, everyone knows everybody all the time.

—A live church is always changing its methodology; a dead church never has to.

A Model for Action

We find even better principles of adjustment in Christ. Crowds were always creating problems for him; yet no situation every got beyond his compassion. He was always receptive to every need and every person.

Mark 4 gives an incident that reflects Christ's willingness to accommodate himself to any need. Assembled at lakeside, the crowd pressed upon him until he could no longer speak where he was standing. Entering a boat, he pushed away from the shore and continued speaking from there. He let his preaching style meet the need of the growing crowd. He did not ask the crowd to accommodate him.

Jesus wanted people to be themselves. He loved each one for his or her unique personality traits. His choice of the disciples reflects his desire that people fulfill their own spiritual destinies.

We do not read where Jesus ever asked one disciple to be like another. He did not say to Simon, "You need to be like Andrew; less impulsive and more dependable." He never told Philip that he needed to be more active, like Simon; nor did he ever tell Thomas that he wished one time he would take him at his word as John did. Jesus never compared one to the other or asked one to copy another. He allowed each of them to mature in the strength of his own personhood.

Each individual in a growing church needs to feel the worth of his or her unique gifts. Each must be allowed to serve through the integrity of his or her own personality. Affirming persons for what they are and helping them serve as they are crucial ingredients for guiding church growth.

One further ingredient for guiding church growth is forgiveness. You cannot rub shoulders without getting an occasional elbow. You will need to be willing to forgive when you do.

Three ministers went to see a senator. They asked him to talk about compassion.

Picking up a pencil, he said, "Gentlemen, look at this pencil. Just as the eraser is only a very small part of the pencil and is used only when you make a mistake, so compassion is only called upon when things get out of hand. The main part of life is competition, only the eraser's compassion."

After the interview, one of the ministers confided that for him the beauty of Christianity is that it is all eraser. We need that spirit. The need is not so much to convict people of their sin as it is to convince them of their forgiveness. We can turn crowds into congregations as we become less competitive and more compassionate.

Causing church growth, however, is part of the responsibility placed upon us by the Great Commission. Christ's vision of the world is meant to open our eyes to our part of the world too. This challenge for the world should make us effective in our own community, as well as supportive of missions in all the world.

Some years ago, Glendon McCullough participated in a unique service of ordination. A German-speaking congregation had called one of their own young men to become their pastor, and Glendon had consented to preach the ordination sermon. The church was about thirty years old, but the young man would be their first pastor. How the church began and how that young pastor related to that beginning made the ordination service unique.

One lady had sensed the need for a church among her fellow Germans. She began to teach Sunday School in her home. Later, they were able to buy some land and erect a little prefab building, but they were never able to call a pastor. Meanwhile, the lady kept praying that God would send them a pastor and continued to give what leadership she could.

Years later, a teenage boy came forward in one of the services, saying that God had called him to preach. As he prepared for the ministry, it occurred to the church that part of his preparation could be his service among them as their pastor. While he was learning, he could also practice. Since they had no pastor, the relationship would help them as well as him. So they called him to become their first pastor.

It was a proud day. Other Baptist leaders were invited to share the celebration. Here is what made the service unique: the young man being ordained to the ministry was the grandson of the lady who had helped start the church! Her prayers had been answered. Her own grandson became the pastor for whom she had prayed so long.

That year, McCullough was invited to speak to an assembly of Baptist leaders in that same state. He decided to share the story of that ordination. He referred especially to the faith of the grandmother, calling careful attention to the thirty years in which she never ceased praying for her church and for a pastor.

Glendon then asked, "Where were you during those thirty years? Was there no one of you who felt any burden for that church? Did you even know about it?"

This is not meant to diminish the beauty of how God answered the prayers of that dear lady. It is a valid reminder, however, that many times the needs closest to us are not met because we do not see them. We share Christ's vision best when we see all the needs of the world, particularly those near enough to us to fill.

I read a story somewhere about a lady's dream. She was looking out on a vast crowd of people. All of them were reaching toward her, longing for some response that she knew them and cared for them. In her dream, she said, "Lord, I want to reach out and touch them all! But there are so many. What shall I do?"

When she awoke, she still remembered the answer she was given. God had said, "Touch those whom you can reach!"

3
Confessional Preaching
John R. Claypool

It seemed appropriate to me, given the subject I was assigned, to begin with a brief confession of how I began to preach confessionally. This was not a methodology that I was taught by my academic mentors, nor do I recall having it modeled for me in the early days of my professional formation. If anything, this style of proclamation was actually frowned upon. The few times confessional material did appear in a sermon, there would always be the disclaimer, "Please pardon the personal reference." I realize why this methodology was shunned and shall attempt to deal with it later. The point I am making now is that I literally stumbled into this mode of preaching quite unintentionally.

My first experience of confessional preaching, I remember, was during the days I was the assistant pastor at the First Baptist Church of Decatur. I was doing a series of Sunday night sermons aimed at the specific problems facing the youth of that day. When it came time to address the issues of faith and doubt, I decided to recount my journey out of innocence into secondhand faith through the void of not knowing until truth really did begin to happen for me as an adult. There was an electric quality to that particular part of the sermon. All of you here know what I am talking about—those all too rare moments when, to use Paul Scherer's term, "it sung." I was very aware of this and also impressed by some things that happened subsequently.

In the next few days, no less than ten folk made appointments to come by and talk and began by saying, "I heard you say the other night that you had trouble believing. I'd like to talk some more about that." This, of course, is one of the serendipitous facets of the act of preaching. It does create a certain image of the proclaimer which can either open or close subsequent doors of ministry. People do not just hear the sermons we preach; they are also sizing up our competence and trustworthiness and often make up their minds whether they want to entrust their deeper selves to intimate interaction with us by virtue of the sermon. Wayne Oates used to say that no preacher is ever paid a higher compliment than having some frightened, timid soul come up after a sermon and say quietly, "I wonder if I could speak with you privately about certain things that are a deep concern to me?" My point is that the unveiling of my personal struggle with doubt and faith seemed to connect with other doubters. It took the shame and isolation out of a certain kind of experience and opened the way for future sharing.

I moved to Crescent Hill in October 1960 and within the first months there had occasion to use a variation of that sermon and had the same thing happen. Folk who were struggling with their own experiences of doubt sought me out because of what I had shared. The interesting thing to me now is that these two experiences did not register more deeply on me or alter my preaching style. Although I was impressed by these phenomena, I do not recall utilizing this strategy more often.

Some years later I did share some of my own struggles in coming to positive self-esteem, but it was not until July 1969 that a family tragedy set the stage for me really to experience the power of confessional preaching. As some of you may remember, this was the time when my eight-and-a-half-year-old daughter was diagnosed as having leukemia. I got the fateful word on a Wednesday afternoon and made no attempt to preach the following Sunday. But some eleven days after this word, I entered the pulpit with the awareness that everyone in the congregation knew what had happened to us and what I had been doing with the past few days of my life. It seemed to me that there was nothing else to do in that moment but share with my family in Christ some of my own reflections on the events of those days. And this is what I did. I preached two other sermons in a similar vein in the next eighteen months—one after Laura Lue had relapsed from her first remission and then a sermon some five or six weeks after her death. Those three preaching events opened my eyes as never before to the authentic potency of letting what has happened to you begin to happen through you as you honestly share it with other people. It was at this juncture of my career that I began to reflect on this whole methodology of regarding one's own experiences—both positive and negative—as a resource for preaching.

That was some twelve years ago now, and in this intervening period I have thought a great deal about this approach to preaching, and I would like to identify several conclusions to which I have come.

Three Positive Conclusions

As I began to reflect critically on this methodology, I discovered three positive things about confessional preaching. First of all, it was consistent with one of the primal images Jesus used in commissioning his followers for the post-ascension phase of his ministry. "Ye shall be witnesses unto me" (Acts 1:8), Jesus said, to the whole world. What is a witness? It is a law court image. A witness is a person who is placed under oath and then invited to tell as honestly and completely as possible his or her own experience of a given event. The task of the witness is not to climb into the jury box and force his or her interpretation on other people. No, the sole responsibility of a witness is to describe honestly his or her personal experience of a given process.

Jesus did not begin to commission witnesses after his resurrection. Recall his remarkable encounter with the Gadarene demoniac (Luke 8:26-39). My most recent mentor, Myron Madden, suggests that this man's problem, in all likelihood, was unresolved grief. Jesus found him literally beside himself in a cemetery. Madden speculates that he had experienced some kind of loss and could not come to terms with it. He was literally immobilized in a graveyard. Jesus came and opened the way for him to get things together and let go the past and move into the future with courage and hope. What a great ministry to perform for any "person of sorrow, acquainted with grief!" Understandably, the healed griever wanted to stay with the

Source of his healing. But Jesus said, "No, go back to your own region and tell folk there what the Lord has done in and for you." That was confessional preaching, if you please, sharing with others those realities that are saving you. This is what it means "to bear witness." I was amazed when I began to reflect how old and central such a procedure has always been in Christian history.

That insight led me on to realize that this was a methodology that Paul also utilized extensively in his work. Someone asked me once why the story of Saul's conversion on the Damascus road is related in detail three times in the Book of Acts (9:1-9;22:6-16;26:12-18). My spontaneous reply was because he probably told it three thousand times! My hunch is that everywhere the great missionary statesman went, he began by saying, "Let me tell you how I got into this business in the first place. Here is what happened to me. Perhaps this can become the beginning point of what can happen to you as well." Those of you who are students of the Pauline literature realize that not just the event on the Damascus road but many other experiences were called into the service of Paul's proclamation—his "thorn in the flesh" (2 Cor. 12:7-10), his encounter with Peter (Gal. 2:11-14), his shipwrecks and beatings (2 Cor. 11:23-33). He made what happened to him a vehicle of what might happen through him.

These biblical precedents led me to a third conclusion: confessional preaching is true to the incarnational principle that seems to be one of God's primary ways of doing his work in history. We are all familiar with the affirmation in the prologue to John's Gospel: "the Word became flesh and dwelt among us" (1:14, RSV). Among other things, this means that God did not keep his distance from us; he really became involved totally in all the agonies of history. As the early church fathers put it, "He became what we are that we might become what he is." And my sense is that confessional preaching is participation in that same form of involvement where the preacher gets down into the very realities that he proclaims to other fellow strugglers. The power of confessional preaching is that it does narrow the distance between the pulpit and the pew. It assumes the stance of "the inclusive we" rather than "the over against you," and this form of communication does have potency, not just in preaching but in all forms of relationships.

John Powell, the Jesuit priest out of Loyola in Chicago, identifies four levels of communication in his well-known little book, *Why Am I Afraid to Tell You Who I Am?*[1] The first level is what he calls "cliche communication." This is the ritualizing we do on elevators and at receptions and parties where nothing really significant is intended or expected; it is simply a way of handling superficial relationships. The second level is what he calls "sharing facts or information about people and subjects." At its worst, it takes the form of gossip; at its best, it can be disinterested inquiry about a commonly held subject. The third level is when you share your own ideas, opinions, and judgment about things. You are no longer simply sharing information objectively, but you risk your own interpretation of this information with another.

The fourth level Powell identifies is when you "share your own feelings, how all of this strikes you and where you are in relation to it." This is "gut-level communication" to use Powell's term, and this is where authentic intimacy is to be found. I would suggest that confessional preaching comes closest to this fourth level of communication. You could take these levels and probably remember sermons you have heard or perhaps preached that fall into each category. However, confessional preaching is "struggling with the angel" as Jacob did (Gen. 32:22-32). When this happens, the preacher becomes a participant and not a spectator in the process he is addressing, and a certain urgency, an existential vitality enters that simply does not exist at other levels of communication.

I remember hearing Harvey Cox tell years ago of going into the Army during World War II and being assigned to the paratroop division, although at the time he had never even been up in an airplane. The training program was highly accelerated, being taught by a veteran jumper. Cox reported that nobody had to nudge him to keep him awake during that instruction, for he and all the others knew full well that in a matter of days they were going to be up in an airplane and have to jump. The realization made them hang on every word with vital interest. Cox went on to comment that the trouble with so much of our life in the church is that it does not have that life-or-death urgency about it. We seem to be transferring information that is interesting to know but does not make much difference. What a contrast this is to D. T. Niles's famous image of preaching, which is that of "one starving beggar telling other beggars where he has found bread." When the things that are saving me or the things that are troubling me become the heart of pulpit interaction, there is an involvement, a closing of the distance that seems to me is a valid extension of the incarnational principle. The Word did not just become words. God did not placidly step down out on the ramparts of heaven and talk down his truth to our anguished planet. No, the Word became flesh, got involved with us, plunged into all the ambiguities and agonies that constitute our not-yet-complete creation. And the preacher who plunges into the same chaotic struggle and willingly shares both the light and the darkness that are his or her experience of it is doing something very true, I think, to the pattern of all divine saving.

Some Potential Weaknesses

Here, then, are some of my positive conclusions about the method of confessional preaching. Let me turn now to some of the obvious dangers and potential weaknesses of this approach to preaching. I cannot think of anything in all creation that cannot be misused or overused or wrongly used. Therefore, it does not discredit the approach to recognize clearly that for all its potency, it certainly carries liabilities and perils as well. What are they? Let me use two questions that have always been the classic instruments of ethical analysis; namely, what is one's motive? and what are the likely consequences to result if one acts a certain way?

It is very important to ask of any episode of confessional preaching: why am I doing this? Is it to get something for myself or to give something of myself for the growth and benefit of others? Obviously, confessional preaching could easily become an excuse for exhibitionism, a subtle attempt to draw attention to ourselves for whatever sick need of recognition this might represent. My brilliant successor at Crescent Hill, Stephen Shoemaker, wrote me a very thoughtful response to my Beecher Lectures where I discussed this whole strategy of preaching. He said his uneasiness was that confessional preaching directed the attention of the congregation to the preacher rather than to the drama of the gospel. In such a process, the preacher emerges as either hero or goat, depending upon how he presents himself, and this could be a real diversion from what authentic preaching is all about. I heartily agree with this danger. Reinhold Niebuhr reminded a whole generation of our forebears that our human proclivity to self-serving is virtually unlimited. We are capable of using anything and everything—even the act of preaching—to gain some self-enhancement at the expense of others. And, therefore, anyone who would ever utilize this strategy must be aware of this danger and ask soberly, Am I buying something here, or am I giving something? Is this an expression of "need-love," as C. S. Lewis defines it, that emptiness in me that causes me to reach out to another for the purpose of getting something from that object that I might transfer it back to my own emptiness? This is an extractive, exploitive, manipulative process, and who of us can claim to have been above it always in our preaching?

Why do you quote from Camus or John Updike or Sören Kierkegaard or Karl Barth? Is it simply because in honesty you want to identify where you received a certain truth, or is it to impress your peers that you are conversant with such giants? Confessional preaching is open to the special temptation of being an act of need-love; however, it can also be an expression of gift-love. It can be part of the fullness that a generous, graced preacher is willing to share for the enhancement of others, not their extraction. Therefore, the motive issue is an exceedingly important one for all preaching but certainly for the use of its confessional form.

The other question to ask is, What is the likely consequence of such an action? Here I think we have to be very realistic in saying the possibility of disillusioning and discouraging parishioners is inherent and needs to be taken into account. In my experience with confessional preaching, on more than one occasion, I have had people get upset by my sharing certain shadows and struggles in my experience or downright enraged that I did not accentuate the positive and eliminate the negative. The basic principle of American advertising is to focus exclusively on the positive and exude only a shining image. Thus, we will need to discuss in our dialogue what it does to people in the pew when they hear the spokesperson for a certain ideal acknowledge that he or she has not yet arrived, very much still in the process.

I certainly concede that there are types of experiences and specific individuals where this strategy could be counterproductive for growth. One needs to exercise this form of preaching with as much wisdom as one makes all the distinctions of pastoral practice. However, having recognized this, I would at least raise this question: if we do not ultimately run a greater risk of disillusioning people by attempting to convey a state of perfectionism that is beyond our actual reality? If the preacher can never share any of his incompleteness or "the shadow side" that represents the areas where he has yet to grow, sooner or later these are going to come to light. Then having made no room for such possibilities, this incompleteness may well discourage idealistic folk more than an honest admission of the realities. I have said many times that I think it is very important where in the process of life we positionize the perfect and the ideal. If it is made our omega point, that toward which we strive and by which we evaluate our progress, it has unending power to inspire and to develop and to mature us. But if we ever come to the idea that perfection can be embodied in the midst of the process, or convey to other people that we have "arrived" or that such arrival is a possibility, that, it seems to me, is the seedbed of disillusionment. Process appears to be God's way of growing all things to their fullness: "first the seed, then the blade, and then the flower." All of us are incomplete, not yet being what we have it in us to be. And while one needs to exercise discretion in what one reveals to whom, it seems to me that confessional preaching can take the shame and isolation out of struggle and incompleteness, can give other strugglers companionship in what they face, and in lifting the illusion of perfectionism off their shoulders, can offer a real resource for growth in the way.

Here, then, are my reflections on confessional preaching. This is by no means "the last word" on the subject. It is offered as the first word in an ongoing conversation. Confessional preaching is by no means the only form that authentic proclamation should assume. It is but one tool in the good craftsman's tool chest. No one should use it exclusively; however, my sense is if you never use it, you are overlooking a real potential to bless. The things that have happened to us have great potency when we allow them to happen through us in open sharing.

Note

1. John Powell, *Why Am I Afraid to Tell You Who I Am?* (Chicago: Argus Communications, 1969).

Slow Learners and Hope
Philippians 1:2-11; 3:12-14

Toward the end of his life, C. S. Lewis wrote that, from time to time, he had experiences which made him realize that "the progress he thought he had made religiously was largely imaginary, and that the real work of redemption was still to be done." I can really identify with such a statement, for as recently as last week, in getting back from my study leave and preparing for the first Sunday, I had just such "a moment of truth."

Those of you who have been around me much have probably heard me talk of my own particular journey of faith. Like any little child, I started out as "a keen observer but poor interpreter." Early in my pilgrimage I came to two crucial conclusions about reality. For one thing, I did not see any value whatsoever in myself as I existed at the moment; and second, I thought if I were ever going to have value, I had to go outside myself and acquire it by energetic effort. "If you are ever going to amount to anything, you must make something of yourself" was the dictum that shaped my earliest perceptions, and it is not surprising, given such assumptions, that I grew into an anxious, driven, competitive type of person who was forever trying to make a name for himself by what he did so as to fill that awful vacuum of emptiness at the center of his being.

Across the years I have spent a lot of energy trying to ascertain why I came to those particular conclusions about reality; frankly, all this "archeological exploration" into my past has produced no conclusive results. It is still largely a mystery to me exactly why I saw myself as a nobody or why I chose acquisition as a way of life, but that this happened and that it shaped my subsequent development, I cannot deny. And I suppose I would still be nothing more than "<u>homo competitus</u>" if something had not happened to me in the middle of my fourth decade that proved to be the most revolutionary event since my birth. I have shared before the details of this experience and I shall not repeat all of them. Suffice it to say, I found myself one Tuesday morning in the office of a Presbyterian minister friend because he had had the courage to acknowledge his need and reach out for help. "Where does a pastor go for pastoral care?" he had said to me on the phone the day before. "We are so busy meeting everybody else's needs that we never tend to our own."

As a result, six of us clergypersons had convened with no other agenda but being honest with each other, hoping we could build up enough trust so that we could take off our masks and thus be in a position to tend both our own and each other's wounds. It turned out to be a remarkable experience—brand new to me whose seminary training had been solely academic. After a few braver souls had showed the way, I too, one Tuesday morning, took off my mask. For the first time in my life, I acknowledged the sense of nobodiness that went all the way back to the beginning and the desperate efforts to acquire that had been my response to this. Up to that moment, not even I realized the extent of the fear and the hurt and the loneliness that had accumulated across the years. It was like lancing a boil or experiencing extreme nausea; when I had finished, the man in the group with whom I felt the least natural affinity, a wellborn, Episcopal priest, was the first to speak. He said: "I hear you, John, I hear you. That is my story too. Do you know what we need?" I shall never forget that inclusive "we." He did not look down on me and say patronizingly, "Do you know what you need?" There was a brotherly solidarity. "Do you know what <u>we</u> need?" he asked. "We need to hear the gospel down in our guts. Do you remember over in the Sermon on the Mount when Jesus said: 'You are the light of the world?' He did not say: 'You have to be number one in order to acquire light or outachieve everyone to earn light.' No, he said, <u>You are light</u>. If you and I could ever really hear that down in our guts and believe it, then we could do what Jesus said. <u>We could let our light shine</u>, and people could see the good thing that God has created and give glory to the Father in heaven."

I cannot explain to you why I had never "heard" that word of Scripture in my guts before because, God knows, I had read it many times, even in the Greek. All I can report is that in that moment, something like fire moved from the top of my head to the bottom of my heart, and for the first time in my life, grace ceased to be just a word and became an event. My eyes were literally opened to the fact that I had been wrong all along in thinking of myself as a nothing who had to acquire worth by energetic effort. There had been worth placed in me by God from the moment I was created. What God had made of me, not what I had to make of myself, was the crucial issue; suddenly the image of a man "riding on an ox, looking for an ox" became a description of what I had been doing for thirty-five years. There I was looking anxiously in all directions for that which would give me a sense of worth, and all along what I was looking for was right underneath me by grace of creation.

That has to be the most revolutionary single discovery of my life. You talk about "altering or raising consciousness"—I began "to see" all things in a new light. Instead of having to go out and find cards in order to get in on the game of life, I realized I had already been dealt a hand of cards; the agenda was to pick them up gratefully and see how I could play them with relish and abandon. It is one thing to acquire light and try to make a shining place for yourself by strenuous effort. It is another thing altogether to realize that you are light by the grace of creation and are called on solely to let that light shine through you and beyond you. Awareness of what you already have rather than acquiring what you do not have became the real issue, and I repeat: this was a discovery that turned my whole perceptual world upside down. What the Damascus Road encounter was to Saul of Tarsus, this event of grace in the office of a Presbyterian minister was to me.

I almost hesitate to use the words born again to describe that moment, for this term has become so distorted, but I am going to risk it anyway. There are two things about the experience of birth that apply to this particular event. Think about it—at birth, a new thing comes into being. That is the whole wonder of birth. But this new thing is not complete or full-grown in that moment. Whatever is born has to grow and develop through many stages before it comes to maturity. Growth and development have been as real aspects of my experience with grace as was the newness of its coming. One starts out as "a babe in Christ" just as one starts out a babe in physical terms. Thus it is no wonder, a la C. S. Lewis, that we have experiences that make us realize we have not progressed as far as we thought we had, but the real work of being completed in grace is still to be done.

This has certainly been the pattern of my life. What began so dramatically for me back in 1965 has had to grow inch by inch. I did not that morning take off my old reality conclusions like a coat and leave them behind completely. Five years after that experience I came down with hepatitis and was flat on my back for three months, and a depression set in that went beyond the physical debilitation. As I dug into that darkness, I realized it rooted in the idea that, since I was not doing anything of value just then, I felt I had no value. Lo and behold, the old virus of needing to acquire what I did not have rather than being aware of what I did have was still present.

Ten years after that, in fact, just last week, I came face-to-face with it again. I could not have had a better study leave experience, and everyone here was wonderfully warm in welcoming us back. But last Wednesday, Thursday, and Friday, folk would say, "I cannot wait until Sunday to hear what you have to say." I found myself getting more and more anxious and tense. I thought to myself: They are going to expect gold to drop out from my mouth this first Sunday back. If I do not really "hit a home run," they will say: "What has he been doing all these months? Why did we let him off?" Please do not misunderstand me—it was not what you did, but the old virus of needing to acquire worth by what I did that set up this reaction. Now to be honest, this experience caught me by surprise. I thought I had grown beyond that stage, but obviously I have not.

How we choose to respond to such moments of truth about ourselves is very significant. It would be easy to get discouraged over the slowness of our progress. Last week part of me said, What's the use? If after all this time and so much talking about grace, you are still hardly out of square one, is there any hope of total healing?

That temptation was very real, but wait: what held me back was remembering that this event of grace was another form of a birth, and with births there is always incompleteness as well as newness. Whatever is born has to grow inch by inch and step by step. So why should I be surprised that what had begun so vividly was not yet finished? I was greatly heartened at this point by the words of Paul that I read for the text of the morning. They were not written the night after the Damascus Road encounter when old things passed away for Saul and all things became new (2 Cor. 5:17). No, some twenty-five years later at the very end of his life, he could write to the Philippians: I have not yet arrived. "I count not myself to have apprehended: but this one thing I do, forgetting those things which are behind, and reaching forth unto those things which are before, I press toward the mark for the prize of the high calling of God in Christ Jesus" (Phil. 3:13-14). What kept Paul from blowing up in frustration or going down in despair over his slow progress? It was the hope expressed in an earlier part of the letter, that he who had begun a "good work" in him would see it to completion in the Day of Christ (Phil. 1:6). Those last words are the key to when the completion will come, and the dynamism, of course, is the tenacity of God to finish what he started. If we could only remember how God works—through process, not instant creation—it would help so much.

I honestly think that mistaken expectations are the big problem. More often than not, disillusion is the child of illusion; that is, if we start out with the wrong assumptions, we are bound to come to faulty conclusions. When C. S. Lewis was fifteen years old, he went to study with Dr. W. T. Kirkpatrick, who was noted for preparing young men for the exams to get into Oxford or Cambridge. Kirkpatrick was a ruthless logician, who firmly believed that the only legitimate use of the vocal cords was either to communicate or discover truth. He had no patience with small talk or fuzzy thinking. Lewis learned that within minutes after getting off the train. As the two of them were walking along, in an attempt to make conversation, Lewis said, "The scenery here in Surry is wilder than I expected."

The old man turned abruptly and said: "Stop! What do you mean by wildness and what grounds did you have for expecting the scenery to be a certain way? Have you ever been to Surry before? Where did you get the idea that it ought to be a certain way?"

Lewis said that after a few fumbling passes, it was evident that he had no idea of what he meant by wildness and no basis whatsoever for his expectation.

At that point the teacher said: "Your statement then was meaningless. You must learn to encounter realities and then describe them, not build up expectations ahead of time on no basis."

It was a lesson that Lewis carried with him the rest of his life, and all of us would do well to learn it too. Where did the idea ever come from that we should reach total maturity quickly or without lots of falling down and getting up? If we abandon the expectation that our growth should be another way, then we can live into where we are and use it as an occasion to "press on to the mark" as Paul said (Phil. 3:14), rather than giving up in discouragement.

On more than one occasion I heard Dr. Martin Luther King, Jr., close an address with the familiar words of an old slave's prayer: "O Lord, I ain't what I ought to be, and I ain't what I'm gonna be, but thanks be to you, I ain't what I used to be." How true this is to the process nature of our life, and how wise to choose to focus on how far one has already come rather than on how far one has yet to go.

That is the response I chose to make last week when it became clear that the progress I thought I had made was largely imaginary and that the real work of putting off the old way of acquiring and putting on the new way of grace was still to be finished. Discouragement was a real option, but I did not embrace it. Why? I remembered, rather, what I try to get you to remember Sunday by Sunday as you leave, namely, that we are being redeemed. Something was born in me fifteen years ago that was utterly new, but it has not come to full growth yet. Life is not having to acquire what we do not have by frantic effort but becoming aware of what we already have by grace. That ox that I had been looking for is right underneath me and has been all along. I know that, and yet I do not know it completely. So what do I do? Instead of giving up in discouragement and turning back, I choose, like Paul, to press on to "the mark for the prize of the high calling of God in Christ Jesus." To be sure, "I ain't what I ought to be, and I ain't what I'm gonna be," but wait: "I ain't what I used to be," and that is my hope. He who has begun a good work in me will see it to completion in the <u>Day of Christ</u>!

Here then is where I am today—not as far along as I thought but on my way. And the same is true of you as well. I debated whether to preach as I have this morning but decided to for two reasons. I want to seize every opportunity to proclaim the word of grace. It is so hard for folk like us to believe that we already have worth from God and do not have to be more or better or different to get it. Then, too, I thought it might encourage some of you who lament the slowness of your growth to hear another confess that what has begun is by no means finished. Being a slow learner does not disqualify one. It may be death to pride but not to hope. Listen, the issue is not how long it takes us to be fully graced but the trust we have in him who, having begun a good work, will see it through to completion. That we are not yet there does not mean we have not started.

Therefore, take hope—not what we ought to be. Not what we are going to be. And not what we used to be—thanks be to God. We are on the way—let us then grow on!

4

Parabolic Preaching: Perspectives on Life

Peter Rhea Jones

The parables of Jesus were slices of daily life with the kingdom of God providing perspective. Then and now they function as an exegesis of life illuminating personal existence. Some of the parables are pastoral and some prophetic. Some are general situation and others specific situation. They are not merely insightful tales or memorable anecdotes. They offer powerful, compelling perspective on life. Thus the preacher has not only delightful biblical texts conveying all the charm of story, nor only great pronouncements and principles, but rather the distinct opportunity to offer telling illuminations of contemporary life if deftly, pastorally, faithfully explored.

Let's be more specific and suggestive. Consider these perspectives from the parables:

Life in the Light of Grace
Life in the Light of Nature
Life in the Light of a Moment of Truth
Life in the Light of National Religious Crisis
Life in the Light of Death
Life in the Light of the Final Judgment

Put aside your outlines and structures and patterns normally utilized for textbook analyses of the parables and let your imagination go to work freshly asking what perspectives on daily living do the parables in fact provide that will make a difference in the life of my congregation.

Life in the light of grace, for instance, can be glimpsed in the parables of the pharisee and the tax collector and in the parables of the lost in Luke 15. When Grace looked down on two men praying in the Temple, appearances took a pounding and surprising spiritual realities surfaced. Grace shines on worship and revelation happens! Read this parable and others in Clarence Jordan's *Cottonpatch* translation of Luke and Acts. Turn over the very winsome and highly familiar specific situation of the parable of the prodigal son in the light of the compassionate father's receiving of his sinful son and the intentional contrast of the indignant brother refusing to accept.

Life in the light of nature can be drawn from parables such as the mustard seed, the seed growing on its own, and the sower and the soils. Life in the light of a moment of truth interestingly enough can be discovered in the story of the wounded man and the immediate, unpremeditated responses of two clergy and a compassionate Samaritan. Consider also the parable in Matthew 18 concerning the unmerciful servant as a moment of truth.

If this line of thought begins to commend itself, preach also on life in the light of a national religious crisis <u>after</u> you have pondered the hard hitting parable of the barren fig tree and/or the parable of the wicked tenants. Religious leadership then and now, televised and otherwise, must face the judgment of God.

Life in the light of death receives telling illumination in the parables of the rich fool and the rich man and Lazarus. The vantage of death can be a very helpful friend bringing a heightened sense of urgency and responsibility. Death in both parables exposed the superficiality of ephemeral commitments. The threat of death can propel people to get on with lasting achievements before the night falls. Death is a helpful interpreter of life, a kind of hermeneutic of existence. Death exposes the things that matter and the things that last.

And in like manner the great assize or final exam throws light on life. In the parable of the sheep and the goats life is measured by compassionate existence. The parable has great value for creating responsibility for living because as Brunner recognized responsibility is to be summoned and especially to be summoned to give an account of your life before God. The parable relates to the prevailing purposes of an individual's life. When a person meets human need, the acid test appears in the response. A great but meaningful series of sermons could be developed from the perspectives on life provided by the parables of Jesus. Other suggestions follow, including the challenging possibility of parabolic preaching.

Books of Sermons on Parables

Of the numerous books of sermons on the parables, consider several of the stronger ones. They tend on the whole to offer messages on and from the parables. The great set of sermons by Helmut Thielicke, bound under the title of the lead sermon *The Waiting Father,* are sermons proclaimed in Saint Michael's Church in Hamburg before ample audiences. Notable in the light of conscious focus on methodology is his staying with the story. Thielicke does not discern the disclosure and dispense with the narrative. Indeed, it might be said that he gives up homiletical artistry in order to retain the story.

His sermons arise from a strong engagement with life, for Thielicke as person is one who has drunk deeply of life. He constantly speaks to money, technology, sex, and personal relations. This lively dialogue keeps his sermons from parables very much alive. Though Thielicke seeks what he calls the salient point and succeeds in avoiding the parable as moral example, the form often turns into a new-fashioned homily. The sermons are evangelical and apologetic. They are sometimes socially sensitive, and they are consistently in touch with the feelings of emptiness felt by nihilists and the fear felt by the European in the nuclear age. This Spurgeon in academic gowns speaks the language of the street poetically. Yet he abhors spiritual foam and froth. Not for Thielicke is the mood and mist syndrome of some contemporary homiletical fare. "The Word of God, however," says Thielicke, "is not a feast for the ears but a hammer. A man who comes from it unbruised need not think it has taken root in him."[1]

Note that the content of Thielicke's preaching from parables is categorically Christian. Second, the narrative is more or less kept throughout. Third, the language is not prissy or heavily academic. He says himself in the preface, "The language of preaching . . . has cost the author far more effort and difficulty than the 'carpentered' academic form of speech."[2] The book is one of the great moments in homiletical literature. It appeals to the imagination and comes from the imagination and results from digging in the texts, standing under the Word, and living in the world as a participant.

Turn to another master preacher who comes from a psychological orientation in Great Britain rather than from a theological and ethical concern in Europe. In 1944 Leslie Weatherhead put forward *In Quest of a Kingdom* at a time when his church, the City Temple, had been destroyed by enemy action.[3] The book is quite considerable and tends in and of itself to repudiate the suggestion that little of Weatherhead was genuinely substantial or enduring.

Weatherhead centered theologically on the kingdom, a decision that kept his sermons in substance. He sought not only to understand the texts and to illuminate life by their light but also to inspire persons to do something about their message. He, like Thielicke, is quite gutsy and existential, but unlike Thielicke offers many classical illustrations and far more structure. Weatherhead's sermons take the stories seriously and draw insights from them in a progression toward the ending.

Weatherhead, despite his psychological forte and his focus on the individual, evinced quite a deal of social concern. While many books of sermons on the parables fail to deal with social issues and unresponsive political structures, Weatherhead dared to question systems as in his sermon on the parable of the rich fool he called "Treachery to the Kingdom." The sermons do fail at times to close in on the primary point in favor of a kind of abstracting that is more pastorally insightful than exegetically substantive. His own peculiar personal theology often takes over, fascinating in its own way but not obviously derived from the text itself. Perhaps it is fair to say that Weatherhead failed to take sufficiently into account the special nature of parable as such.

Two strengths stand out above all. The first is reminiscent of Thielicke. Leslie Weatherhead had an uncommon grasp of the nature of human life and its struggles, and he had gone far enough in his working with people to find out how the spiritual resources of the Christian faith could actually help and make a difference.

Pastoral ministry in the war had something to do with it as the extreme realities demanded much from the faith. His native ability is another factor to march forward. Method or art will not succeed beyond the God-given gifts devotedly developed. The person and minister he became make his sermons on parables great. It is increasingly evident to me that what the minister is becoming has an enormous effect upon what he or she can share through preaching.

The second strength is interrelated with the first. Weatherhead's illustrations are exceptional. He told stories laden with power. He shared incidents that are definitely inspirational. He reflected on his pastoral ministry and came up with personal stories that smack not only of reality but of basis for hope. Read his sermonic essay on the parables of the seed growing automatically and the mustard seed entitled "How the Kingdom Spreads." The preacher who penned the words believed in the gospel and in the missionary mandate of the church.

Both Weatherhead and Thielicke are masters in their own way of preaching on the parables and can teach our consultation about preaching bifocally out of the pastoral ministry. Neither of them simply collected good material and did a responsible exegesis and constructed a responsible outline.

Parable Series

The parables are immediately attractive for preaching, and series from a limited set is natural. The parabolic sayings in the Synoptics, the parables in the Old Testament, and the parables in the Fourth Gospel should not be overlooked. In the Gospel of John there are thirteen parables which are quite attractive preaching texts. For example, consider the parabolic saying of the night wind. In the meeting of Jesus and Nicodemus, there just may have been a night wind rustling around the area, and Jesus in effect said, "Listen to the wind, Nicodemus. It 'blows where it wills, and you hear the sound of it, but you do not know whence it comes or whither it goes; so it is with everyone who is born of the Spirit'" (John 3:8).

Beyond these possibly forgotten resources consider doing a series from a common metaphor, such as seed or servant. The seed parables focus on the nature and coming of the kingdom of God. John Crossan calls attention to these as parables of Advent, a natural choice for December proclamation.[4] He calls attention to three themes: hiddenness and mystery, gift and surprise, and discovery and joy. There is the joy of finding treasure (Matt. 13:44) and lost coins and lost sheep (Luke 15:1-9).

Crossan also breaks new ground in his analytical study of the numerous master/servant parables and the time of reckoning present in each. I find it interesting to look to the householder parables as basis for a series on the will of God. The parables commonly utilizing the master of the house are theodicies if you please and allow the preacher to cover the kind of ground Weatherhead dealt with in his best selling *The Will of God*.

The actual title householder (oikodespotē) can simply mean house steward but came to be used of a person of considerable authority. For example, in the parable of the tares (Matt. 13:36-43), the landowner's intention was sabotaged by the enemy. He refused to panic. He asserted that later he would separate the wheat from the weeds. This effort to stifle his will would not win. Eschatologically the original intention would be realized and the sabotage activity would utterly fail. In the laborers in the vineyard (Matt. 20:1-16), the authority and fairness of the householder were called in question publicly. He justified his fairness easily, disposing of the complaint by simply pointing out he paid the full day workers a fair day's wage. His expression of his sovereignty is classic: "Am I not allowed to do what I choose?" (v. 15, RSV).

Again, in the parable of the wicked tenants (Mark 12:1-12 and parallels) the owner sent representatives during harvesttime who were badly treated. Undeterred, his intentions unwavering, he dispatched his son. The wicked tenants imagined that they could murder the heir and be sovereign themselves, but the Lord of the vineyard came and gave the vineyard to others (v. 9). The concerted effort to foil the owner of the vineyard failed.

So far, examples have been drawn from three Gospels (John, Matthew, and Mark). The remaining householder parable stands only in Luke. In the parable of the great banquet (Luke 14:16-24), invited guests made excuses and absented themselves. None of them came, but the resourceful master ordered servants to bring others from the streets to the banquet. He intended a banquet. The guest list changed, but a banquet there was!

Once the householder group of parables unified by a master metaphor appears, several patterns can be seen. One important detail in each case is that (1) the master is also called "lord" (kurios). In secular usage, kurios is "the one who has the power to control and give the word." Thus does the householder act, though with flexibility. (2) In each parable, the master's will is challenged and seems on the brink of being thwarted. In each case, the challenge is met, whether from resistance, criticism, opposition, or rejection. The response is even, firm, never impetuous. The householder is never at a loss of words. After each setback, sovereignty or authority is reasserted in a fresh and convincing manner. The master's will will be, but significantly freedom remains. Some refuse to accept the master's will for themselves.

The master should not be simply equated with God, but certainly this figure is intended to point to the sovereignty of God active in the ministry of Jesus. Both Epictetus and Philo apply the term to God, and it is used of Christ (Matt. 10:25). Surely these householder parables concern the will of God and represent answers (theodicies) to genuine questions and hostile criticisms, such as the apparent powerlessness or weakness of God or his seeming injustice. These issues arose from the teaching and action of Jesus, and the householder parables are sensitive responses. They all posit freedom and sovereignty. They indicate that some can resist God's will but that God's will reasserts itself in fresh and final ways. The parables insist on the freedom of grace, God's right to do as he pleases. There is an awesome note regarding the ultimate authority of judgment held by and exercised by the master. These householder parables are overtly kingdom of God oriented.

A second challenging option for a series of a different sort is to pursue select parables as drama. Look to Dan Via and his book *The Parables* in which he forges a creative link between existence and drama.[5] He singles out several parables as tragic, such as

(1) The talents (Matt. 25:14-30)
(2) The ten maidens (Matt. 25:1-13)
(3) The wedding garment (Matt. 22:11-14)
(4) The wicked tenants (Mark 12:1-9)
(5) The unmerciful servant (Matt. 18:23-35)

By "tragic" Via has in mind a downward movement toward catastrophe and the isolation of the person from society. He also singles out several parables as comic, such as the laborers in the vineyard (Matt. 20:1-16), the unjust steward (Luke 16:1-9), and the prodigal son (Luke 15:11-32). By comic, Dan Via simply means an upward movement toward well-being and inclusion.

With some imagination, these very parables could become an attractive series for preaching, for college students, for retreats or camps. A series on the tragic parables could bring a sense of freshness and expectation to worship as well as an acute recognition of the judgment of God.

Another brief series could be developed on discipleship. Three sermons could evolve on three imperatives:

(1) The imperative of forgiveness: unmerciful servant (Matt. 18:21-35);
(2) The imperative of love: compassionate Samaritan (Luke 10:25-37);
(3) The imperative of perseverance: persistent widow (Luke 18:1-8).

For further detail, consult Part IV of *The Teaching of the Parables.*[6]

Yet another miniseries could center on the challenge to decision. Several different kinds of parables could be clustered for distinctive accents. Three sermons could follow on:

(1) Prophetic call for national repentance: barren fig tree (Luke 13:1-9);
(2) Exposure of inauthentic living: rich fool (Luke 12:13-21); consider the question, "Will it matter that I was?"
(3) Evangelistic call to decision: the six brothers (Luke 16:19-31).

Observe that in all three a reorientation is demanded. Repentance, that now infrequently invited response in the modern pulpit, is necessitated in each of these crisis situations. For further development, consult Part II of *The Teaching of the Parables*.[7]

A series of evangelistic sermons could be drawn up from the parables in Luke 15 and 16. The great fifteenth chapter reflects a gospel for the lost. The parables of the lost coin and lost sheep speak to the people of God in terms of the mandate to <u>recover</u> the lost. This divine intention Jesus incarnated in his own ministry of recovering sinners. Like a shepherd he sought the lost sheep. And the extension of the incarnation means that the church must actively seek out the lost and bring them home.

In like manner, the parable of the compassionate father and the angry brother addresses the people of God in terms of the appropriate way to receive the lost. The prodigal found his way home only to be met with mixed reactions. He experienced the acceptance of the compassionate father, the model for receiving sinners. The prodigal's return was met with resolute hostility by his angry brother. This response reflected the critical attitude of scribes and Pharisees and in the church can respond to those too cynical of sinners to seek them or accept them.

And further an evangelistic sermon must be drawn from the prodigal's choice to come home, a vivid, winsome picture of repentance. So repentance is:

(1) a great awakening ("he came to himself"; "he came to his senses" v. 17, GNB)
(2) a returning to the Father ("I will arise and go" v. 18)
(3) a confessing of sin ("Father, I have sinned against heaven and before you" v. 18, RSV)
(4) entering the joy of the kingdom (vv. 20-24)

The evangelistic series might be capped by a call-to-decision sermon taken from the parable of the unjust steward (Luke 16:1-8). The gospel brings a dangerous opportunity, a crisis requiring right action while there is time.

One last suggestion leads toward a praxis. A pastoral series could be projected. Attention could be given to the parable of the persistent widow (Luke 18:1-8) and preach on the theme "Hang in

There," or to the familiar parable of the sower (Mark 4:1-9) and preach for a change on "Managing Despair." Let us follow up the last suggestion by a little direct attention to the sower.

Notes

1. Helmut Thielicke, *The Waiting Father*, John W. Doberstein, trans. (New York: Harper & Row, Publishers, 1959), p. 56.

2. Ibid., p. 13.

3. Leslie Weatherhead, *In Quest of a Kingdom* (New York: Abingdon-Cokesbury, 1944).

4. John Crossan, *In Parables: The Challenge of the Historical Jesus* (New York: Harper & Row, 1973).

5. Dan Via, *The Parables* (Philadelphia: Fortress Press, 1964).

6. Peter Rhea Jones, *The Teaching of the Parables* (Nashville: Broadman Press, 1982).

7. Ibid.

The Compassionate Samaritan
Luke 10:25-37

The second most famous parable, that of the compassionate Samaritan, speaks to us of the exposure of inauthentic religion. Jesus, like other prophets, recognized that not all religion is healthy. Not all religion is good. Some religion is neurotic, and some of it is selfish. This little story of a few verses has inspired the construction of hundreds of hospitals in history. It has caused a kindness every day for the past two millenia—just a story. But it is powerful word of God.

Often in the parables of our Lord there is an exposing and an extolling. There is an exposing of something that is invalid and inauthentic, and there is an extolling of something that is good, and that's what we find in this most familiar of all the parable stories. The story tells of a man traveling the Jericho road, being robbed and beaten, being left half-dead, thrown in a ditch, and then what happens to that situation as the travelers who follow him come by and see him. And so there is a moment of truth each time one of the travelers passes by. We are allowed to see an exposure of religion that is inauthentic, as the priest passes by and as a Levite also passes by. The priest presumably was just coming from the Temple. He had just been in a worship service, and he sees a man who is wounded and in great need; and he passes by on the other side of the road, in that famous wide detour. He was followed by a Levite, and the Levite was a doorkeeper in the house of God, sometimes a gifted Temple singer or a Temple policeman; and he too saw the wounded man and left him on the road, unaided and unattended, though he probably came up a little closer to the wounded man than did the priest.

Now Jesus, in that swift motion of story, exposes invalid religion. And so far as the lifetime of Jesus was concerned, we must recognize that the story was told, not just on any road, but on the Temple road. We must remember that our Savior had decided to go to Jerusalem and that, upon arrival, he would cleanse the Temple. We find him telling an unflattering story about Temple officials. We are reminded that a Samaritan, on the other hand, who came by later and who cared, was not even allowed into the outer Temple—was not allowed into the inner courts of the Temple at all. The Levite would have kept people like the Samaritan out of church.

Jesus is standing in a great succession, the succession of the prophets, and, like certain prophets before him—such as Jeremiah—Jesus recognized a religion that was inauthentic and that could be associated even with the Temple itself. When we define religion strictly in terms of our relationship with God then we have turned religion into a neurotic, selfish reality. Leslie Weatherhead has pointed out that religion becomes neurotic and out of touch with reality when there is no concern for other persons.

The famous theologian from Chicago, Langdon Gilkey, has said that what this parable does is to expose the whole human predicament. There is here a kind of selfishness, a love of self rather than God and of neighbor that loses both self and the other. Now let us admit that there are times when the religious institution fails. There are times when the Temple and the church fail to be what they ought to be. Surely one of the reasons why the priest and the Levite passed by on the other side was because of what was emphasized in the Temple. The right things weren't happening in the Temple. The right things weren't being said in church.

It is altogether possible in a church today to select devotional passages of Scripture carefully and to omit vast portions of the Word of God and to fail to guide and instruct people about the nature of genuine, full orbed Christian faith. And so our religious institutions may fail to minister to the poor. We may not bother to understand what it is like to be unemployed. We may have the difficulty of not being willing to go out of our way in order to help and to care. There is a risk of being very active in religion in a selective and selfish fashion and developing a personal religion that is neurotic and unhealthy and lacks the vigor the Nazarene would give it. The parable portrays in a critique of religion a prophetic protest against invalid forms of religious institutions.

It's easy enough for us to say that we as religious persons care and that we as religious institutions care—that theoretically and in the abstract we care about humanity and the world and world peace and world hunger. But it's another thing for us to take off our turbans and clean wounds. It's another thing for us to allow someone to ride on our mount. I like the story Bruce Narramore tells about a man who was thought to be a friend of children. Children really were attracted to him, and he seemed to enjoy them; but one day he laid out a lot of fresh concrete and when he got there the next morning there were initials, names, and inscriptions marked into the fresh cement. He blew his cool. He was ranting and raving, angry as could be. He said, "Just wait until I find the kids who did this!"

One of his friends said, "Hey, I thought you liked kids!"

He responded, after thinking a minute, "I like them in the abstract. I don't like them in the concrete!" Sometimes we too like kids and the wounded and the hungry in the abstract, but not in the concrete.

Now the great parable of the compassionate Samaritan exposes inauthentic religion, and we've got our share of it today. But I want to say at the same time that this great parable extols authentic religion. It extols religion like that of the compassionate Samaritan. It gives us a picture of what genuine religion is. We visualize this man responding, caring, lifting the victim, putting him on his beast to ride, taking him to the nearest inn, caring for him through the night. There is the beautiful possibility implied that the Samaritan stayed up all night nursing a stranger back to health. He also gave some money to help defray the additional costs and promised that he would return.

Let us notice something: this is a traveling salesman story. Not the normal traveling salesman story. Notice that it's the story of a commercial figure—a businessman. Let us observe that it is the story of a businessman who is a good man. Frankly, at the expense of the clergy, this businessman is affirmed. He was someone who could get things done; he was a businessman with a heart. And we need businessmen and businesswomen today who can be like the Samaritan, who are willing to go out of their way, even to lose a sale, in order to help a wounded stranger. And there are some select Christian businessmen and businesswomen in our world today and others in the making.

We also discover in the story the answer to the famous question, "Who is my neighbor?" pursued by the persistent lawyer, answered by Jesus in a story. A kind of breakthrough occurred as his question was posed. The answer to "Who is my neighbor?" could be said to be "everyone." It could certainly be said that one's neighbor even includes your enemy, as in this story. But let us try a more literal answer. Let us take an answer no more complex than what is indicated in the story line. Our neighbor is anybody who is wounded. In the parable it is the stranger, the anonymous individual, the "certain man" who has been wounded, who is the object of the compassion and the expression of the authentic religion.

Let us just follow out the obvious. Who are our neighbors? Those who need clothes. Perhaps their clothes have been stolen or they have no other clothes to wear. Who are our neighbors? Those without funds, who need money, whose money has been taken away or lost. Who are our neighbors? Those who are left in the ditches of life. Who are our neighbors? Those whose health may be impaired, those who may be suffering from physical wounds. Who are our neighbors? Those who are neglected, like the aged, like the refugees, whom someone called "the delayed pilgrims," like the runaway daughter or like the alcoholic, or like that teenager who is not accepted into the teenage group because of the clothes she wears. Who are our neighbors?

And what are we to do as neighbors? Clear enough. We ought to offer shelter; we ought to take them to the nearest inn. We ought to accept them as our responsibility. What should we do? We should give the wounded food to eat. That happens to be a challenge at the moment in the city of Atlanta, for there is a need for a soup kitchen in Techwood Village, in downtown Atlanta, and for Christian people to volunteer a night out of the month when they would be willing to serve sandwiches and soup and to express love and interest for the needy people.

Indeed, what are we called upon to do? We are called upon to give hands-on care, not simply to dial the phone and dispatch an ambulance to pick up a person, as important as that may be, but hands-on care. Let us hear this parable if we have ears to hear. There is a call to medical missions. There is a call here for some nurses and doctors to give of their skills in home missions, in foreign missions, in the Third World. For who is our neighbor? Those who are wounded. And through this parable we are called in this hour. What do we need to do as neighbors? We need to provide transportation for those who need our help and support. Indeed, we get a clue as obvious as the story itself. Who is our neighbor? Anybody who is wounded. And how can we respond? We should respond even as the Samaritan responded.

The famous psychologist Adler had a theory he called "the geometry of love." What it amounted to was a theory about distances. Adler's idea was that the way we move toward and the way we move away from people tells a lot about who we are. Our movement toward indicates friendliness and interest and other aspects of love. But moving away from people indicates hostility and anger or negative emotions that we have not resolved. We can tell a great deal about who we are becoming by observing our own movements toward and away from people. Now that may not be obvious to us about our own personal actions; it may be a little subtle. But there are those observers who can tell by looking. Our movement toward and our movement away from people reveal our ability to love. Rollo May has picked up this idea and carried it forward. He has suggested that the person who has real health of personality is someone who can move toward people, someone who has developed the ability to love and to care, and not someone who slips away and avoids other people. Neither of these great psychologists applies his insight to the parable. But don't you see it already? Think about the priest and the Levite who walked by on the opposite side. You see their inability to love as they move away from the wounded stranger, much more concerned about themselves. And you can consider the robbers. Yes, they moved toward him initially, but for hostile reasons. They took what he had and then they too walked away and left him to die. They demonstrated a failure to love.

On the other hand, there was the good Samaritan, who had developed the capacity to move toward a person, in an open-armed, healthy kind of loving compassion. Now look at your own life sometimes. Look at your own movement. Do you move toward people? Do you move away from people? Have you developed some ability to love?

Put it another way. Look again at the familiar story. What are the values displayed by the characters? Consider the worth of the stranger. What is this stranger really worth? Observe the actions of the people in the story. What was he worth to the robbers? His worth to the robbers was only in terms of monetary value. The only value this human being had was monetary: his clothing, his purse. The thieves couldn't care less whether he lived or died. They brutalized the stranger. And what about the priest and the Levite? They valued themselves more than they valued him. But the Samaritan loved and valued the wounded man as much as he loved and valued himself. He would risk for a stranger. And what of our own values? You and I may remember the person whom we have willfully hurt. We may think again of the person intentionally avoided. Or you may also think about that person toward whom you have stretched your hands and your heart and your love. We should be able to see our own values as we read this parable.

We have been reminded that compassion is as concrete as the cross, and compassion is a verb, something that you do. Let us not forget that compassion includes "a tingling sensation in the gizzards." A part of what compassion is is feeling. A part of compassion is to let ourselves feel the hurts and the wounds of other people. It isn't all bad that a little girl cries when her little kitty cat dies. Some of us, perhaps men particularly with the stereotypical expectations placed on us, may have felt the necessity to repress our feelings until they have become like volcanic rock. We are invited, like the

Samaritan, to get in touch with our feelings and our concerns and our love for people other than ourselves.

A mother sent her small daughter to the store to buy a spool of thread. She was gone too long, and her mother wondered what took her daughter so long. When the little girl finally came home, her mother demanded an explanation. Her daughter tried to explain. She said, "My little friend down the street broke her doll, and so I stayed with her."

Her mother was a little put out, and she said, "What could you do for her?"

The child said, "Oh, I sat down and I helped her cry." Sometimes the most compassionate thing you and I can do is to sit down and help somebody cry.

The parable displays inauthentic, selfish, introverted religion. And it extols authentic religion that involves loving God and loving your neighbor as yourself.

Now we have said virtually nothing about the Teller of the story— Jesus of Nazareth. The older interpreters used to say that Jesus was the good Samaritan. Our better understanding of the story would not allow us to say so from an interpretive standpoint, but evangelically it is true. For didn't Jesus become for you and for me the good Samaritan when his compassion became as concrete as a cross and when he healed our wounds by his loving death on Calvary? He invites us to respond to his love. He invites us to allow ourselves to get involved, to be Samaritans.

5

Ethical Dimensions of Preaching

Cecil E. Sherman

Introduction

When ethical preaching is considered, there comes to mind an ethical preaching checklist. This checklist would be divided along theological lines. For the theological conservative, the checklist might include sermons on alcohol, abortion, Sunday observance, and sexual sins. For the liberal, the list might include sermons on hunger, race, ecology, and peace. I could speak to you today about ways to preach on ethical issues. This is one way to go at this assignment.

But I think this is the wrong way to go at ethical preaching. What I have to say to you comes from a pastoral point of view. It has been evolving over an extended course of time. I have served my church for a long time. My purpose in preaching to those people is, by the grace of God, to change them. It seems to me that I change them the more and I change them for the better when I take the long look. I am not trying to reorder their lives with one sermon. Rather, I am trying to amend the way they think; cause them to ponder that which to this point has been taken for granted; get them to see for the first time that part of the Bible that to this time has been hidden. If this comes to pass, then these people will see a part of God they have not yet seen. We become like the God we worship. God is ethical. The more clearly we see the ethical God of the Bible, the more ethical we are likely to become. I have just stated the underlying thesis of such ethical preaching as I do. So how should we preach on ethical matters?

I. Ethical Preaching Is Basic.

Sometimes I hear faint suggestions to the point that ethical preaching is not at the heart of the gospel. The suggestion is that it is peripheral, tangent to the substance of the gospel. This is wrong. Let me illustrate:

—Why are people hungry? All manner of answers have been given to the question. They are hungry because they are lazy. They are hungry because they live in a country that does not have an advanced agricultural education system. They are hungry because they have not enough capital to invest in tools and fertilizers. People much wiser than I tell us that none of these answers is correct. People are hungry because other people are greedy. And why are people greedy? Because they are sinners. So to preach on the "problem of hunger" in depth is to address the sin problem of greed. This is not peripheral preaching. It is at the heart of the gospel.

—Why are people racist? It seems to me that people who are racist have a flawed perception of the nature of God. These people are still trapped in a God who is the "god of my tribe." A universal God who created all, who made all to be brothers and sisters, who reaches toward all in Christ—this God has not yet been seen. To preach on the nature of God is not playing around the corners of the gospel; it is of the essence of it. So, ethical preaching is preaching on basics.

If ethical preaching is to do its real work, a certain kind of person has to issue from such preaching. Let me try to line out the kind of human being our church is trying to shape:

—A sensitive person. Without sensitivity all ethical preaching will fall on deaf ears. So preach for a sensitive human being and you have laid the ground work for all sorts of correct, Christlike ethical response. For example, a sermon about Dives and Lazarus must call attention to the rich man who lived out his days with a beggar at his door. There is no record in the text that the rich man ever noticed the poor man. Such insensitivity is the kind of sin that put him in "torment" (Luke 16:19-31).

—A <u>fair</u> person. Unfairness seeks advantage; fairness does not. God is fair. Peter came to see this in Acts 10. About race he said: "I now realize that it is true that God treats everyone on the same basis" (Acts 10:34, GNB). It is this fairness principle that opens the door to all sorts of right ethical responses.

—A <u>grateful</u> person. Gratitude suggests that we are a beholden, obligated people. The idea of beholdenness is paramount in the Lord's Supper. We are to remember how much Christ has done for us. Paul came to this idea and said, "You do not belong to yourselves but to God; he bought you for a price" (1 Cor. 6:19-20, GNB). When we are grateful, we are conditioned to see ways to repay God by helping the predicament of God's other children.

—A <u>persistent</u> person. Change is never easy. The more we try to change the nature of people, persuade people against their own best interests, the more we are getting into hard work. To do hard work takes a persistent soul, one who is geared up for the long pull. A text that comes to mind is found in Luke 18:1-8. A widow bothered an unjust judge until he set right her case. He did not help her because he was good; he helped her because she was persistent. "Even though I don't fear God or respect men, yet because of all the trouble this widow is giving me, I will see to it that she gets her rights" (Luke 18:4-5, GNB). Fighting greed, advantage, the warrior spirit, the life out of control—this kind of work takes persistence.

—A <u>realistic</u> person. Much unreality has been given to good, church people. I was told when I was a college student that I was to go out and "win the world to Jesus." This was a well-intentioned word; it was also an unrealistic word. For Paul saw the problem more clearly. He said, "We are not fighting against human beings, but against the wicked spiritual forces in the heavenly world, the rulers, authorities, and cosmic powers of this dark age" (Eph. 6:12, GNB).

I recall 1969 when our country put a man on the moon. Soon after, a civil rights leader called for the country to stamp out hunger just as we had mobilized to put a man on the moon. To put a man on the moon was primarily a problem of metals and fuels. To deal with hunger was a matter of changing human nature. This is where God must help else we fail. It takes some realism to do this kind of work. We are signed on for a war that will not end in our lifetime, yet we are not to be discouraged.

—A heavenly person. Only by bringing eschatology into view can one go about the work of doing good with hope. We are not going to win our wars for God. We are going to do our part in a long, unending battle. But all of this has been foretold. "It was in faith that all these persons died. They did not receive the things God had promised, but from a long way off they saw them and welcomed them, and admitted openly that they were foreigners and refugees on earth" (Heb. 11:13, GNB).

When the Spirit of God uses our preaching to produce sensitive, fair, grateful, persistent, realistic Christians who have heaven in view, then our ethical preaching on specific issues will take root and grow. Until then, such ethical preaching we do will probably have superficial effect.

II. Ethical Preaching Is Process.

The object of ethical preaching is to move people along in a lifelong process. To have a yardstick before you will give you some idea of what I am getting at. Can you move your people onward and upward? This is the preacher's work. Let me give you a way to think:

—Some of my people are pagans. They hear me preach, but they live like untamed savages. They break the Ten Commandments. They miss the spirit of the prophets. They cannot even imagine the ways of Jesus.

—More of my people are legalists. They have taken to heart the words of Moses. They have been led out of Egypt, across the wilderness; they have come to Sinai in their ethical pilgrimage. So they do not kill; they do not steal. They usually do not commit adultery. They have a sort of guilt-ridden sense of obligation about their parents. Though they are members of a Baptist church, they function as if they were Old Testament people. They are legalists. Do not look down upon these people. They have begun a journey; no longer are they pagans. They have moved up to legalism.

—A few of my people have begun to taste, sample the radical ethic of Jesus. This minority struggles not to be angry with the brother, not to lust, to do good for evil, and to pray for the enemy (see Matt. 5:21-48). These people are few; many church people dismiss such radical ethic as a "kingdom ethic." That is, such radical ethic is not even to be practiced in this age. We go to great lengths to reduce our obligations, relieve our tensions.

It seems to me that the process ought to be taken in the biblical way. From pagan to legalist to radical Christian is the right course. Trying to shortcut the process leads to some strange types. I have seen some people who have given witness that they have become radical Christians without going through the tedious process of legalism. They just jumped straight from paganism to being radical Christians, but I think this is a hazardous way to go.

About ten years ago in our church family was a high school senior. She was very bright. Her family had reared her in the church. She had heard the radical word about brotherly love. She was against the Vietnam War. She was for feeding the hungry. She was pro black. She was into ecology. But this same girl was at war with her parents; she was pregnant by a black man. All authority was her enemy. Her good mind had turned from her studies. She had none of those legalistic disciplines that are so necessary to the building of an orderly life. She wanted the radical ethic without the Sinai ethic. Being a Christian is a blending of Old Testament and New Testament ways in a mix that leaves duty, obligation, sensitivity, and discipline in place. Beware trying to take people from paganism to Jesus without stopping along the way at Sinai. (Of course, therein is another risk. Some people will follow you to Sinai and no further; our churches are filled with such.)

As you work with your people on a long-term plan of ethical preaching, keep in mind what you are trying to do with them. You are trying to push them upward in a process. Ethical preaching is a process.

III. Ethical Preaching Is Expanding.

Baptists are peculiarly vulnerable to the sin of helping people into the church but not reordering their lives. This is a risk that is built into our strength. We are the people who have kept evangelism alive. We stress calling people to faith. By stressing the call to faith, we are vulnerable to omit the call to holy living. So our churches have more than their share of people who are "saved" but not sensitive, fair, grateful, persistent, and so forth. Jesus has saved their souls but not their lives.

When our churches house these people, we are gathering "latter-day Jews." These people have heaven by dent of a relationship rather than a performance. This was the Jewish sin in the time of Jesus. Often Jesus met people who declared that they were Abraham's children. Because they were lineal descendants of Abraham, they were secure in their relationship with God. Jesus wrestled with these people. They never did hear him very well. Now we have our own sort of Abraham's children: we are saved because we have a relationship to Christ. This relationship covers all. We may rest secure.

There is some truth in what we have told people. A relationship to Christ is basic to salvation, but that relationship must issue in an ethical life. This also is a part of the New Testament. Troubling is Matthew 25:31-46. There Jesus tells the story of the final judgment. The condition for entrance into heaven is stated:

> "I was hungry and you fed me, thirsty and you gave me a drink; I was a stranger and you received me in your homes, naked and you clothed me; I was sick and you took care of me, in prison and you visited me." The righteous will then answer him, "When, Lord, did we ever see you hungry? . . . " The King will reply, "I tell you, whenever you did this for one of the least important of these brothers of mine, you did it for me!" (Matt. 25:35-40, GNB).

To say the same thing again, when Jesus came to the conclusion of the Sermon on the Mount, he added the paragraph about the two house builders. "So then, anyone who hears these words of mine and obeys them is like a wise man" (Matt. 7:24, GNB). The current orthodoxy would change these words to the following: "So then, anyone who hears these words of mine and <u>believes</u> them is like a wise man."

I have no desire to get into a theological war. One may dismiss my arguments as weak, but dismissing the plain sense of the Gospels seems to me to be putting aside our highest authority. These passages put the ethical life in the center of "being a Christian." The place of ethic expands as we grapple to get hold of the gospel.

But it is right at this point that a question has to be asked: <u>which ethical God do we serve?</u> In the same Bible God is described as an exclusive God who cared for the Hebrews more than he cared for the people of Jericho and a universal God who cares for all people regardless of tribe or clan. What part of the Bible we preach tells everything about our perception of the gospel.

We have come upon a time when honest preachers open the Bible and preach a sub-Christian gospel. These people are describing the God of the Hebrews; they hardly know the God of Jonah much less the God of Paul. Our knowledge of God is progressive, expanding. So out of the Bible one may preach the vindicative God of Joshua or the forgiving God of Jesus, the capricious God of Moses or the loving God of the apostle John.

The thoughtful interpreter ought to push toward the expanding ethic of Jesus rather than linger in the smaller, limited, tribal ethic of Moses or Samuel. I understand the necessity of some legalistic preaching. Pagans are moving up when they come to legalism. But push on. Expand the ethical demand as the gospel expands. Keep driving your people further and further into the Bible. If we go far enough, we will take our people to the Cross and to the Sermon on the Mount. None of us has lived life at so exalted a plane, but that is where the Bible would take us. And when such noble living is not found in us, we will be careful to keep the vision of God's intention before the people. It is that vision that pulls all of us upward, higher toward what Christ was and what he meant us to be. This is the expanding ethic, the consuming ethic that lifts the church and makes of us all the salt and light Jesus told us to be (see Matt. 5:13-16).

The Pharisee and the Tax Collector
Luke 18:9-14

Introduction

Jesus lived his life and did his mission in a strange religious setting. Most of the people were casually orthodox. They had religious labels, but their religion did not order their lives. Big holidays and personal moments: this was the sum of their commitment. This is not very different from today. Most of the people around us have some formal religious commitment. Ask them. They will tell you, "I am a Baptist" or "I am a Presbyterian." In fact, religion has little to do with the way they order their lives. The morality of the community is the yardstick these people use when they decide what they will do and what they will not do. Since the yardstick has been getting shorter and shorter for the past few decades, there is more and more that has become permissible. So we live in a "permissive society." Jesus would be at home with us. He lived among such a people. And interestingly, "the common people heard him gladly" (Mark 12:37).

But alongside the great mass who was casually religious, there was a minority who was earnestly religious. These people were of the party of the Pharisees. Nearly all of our references to Pharisees are negative. They are the "bad guys" of the New Testament. This sermon will not change this estimate, but I hope that I can temper it with some understanding of who the Pharisees were and what they stood for in the Jewish community.

Some two hundred years before Jesus, Palestine was ruled by a Syrian king named Antiochus Epiphanes. This man had no respect for the religion of the Jews. He did all he could to persuade the Jews to abandon their religion. In an act that was unspeakably profane,

Antiochus Epiphanes ordered his soldiers to kill a pig on the high altar of the Temple. If you understand the Jewish aversion to swine, you have some idea of just how irreverent, how intolerant, how insulting Antiochus Epiphanes was.

But when the ruler of the land was doing all he could to keep the Jews from their ancient faith, there sprang up from among the people a small set of the faithful. They would be known as Pharisees. These few, at great peril to themselves, vowed a vow. They would be true to the laws of Moses no matter what the cost. At the time, the Pharisees were heroic. They risked themselves for high causes. Most of the populace caved in to the bullying king. A brave few stood fast. It would be around people like the Pharisees that the nation would rally in better days, and the faith of the fathers would make a comeback. I have told you of the first Pharisees.

Two hundred years passed. The sons of the Pharisees did not forget their heritage. At considerable inconvenience and for no small price, the Pharisee practiced his religion. He took it seriously. A Pharisee would not cheat on his wife. A Pharisee would not pad his expense account. A Pharisee would not work on Sunday. A Pharisee would pay all of his taxes. A Pharisee would work at rearing his children in the ways of God. A Pharisee would study his Scriptures. A Pharisee would give to the Temple a full tithe of all he earned. A Pharisee would not forget his prayers.

If all this be so, then what went wrong? Why would Jesus criticize the Pharisees? Therein hangs a tale, a tale that is as applicable today as in the time of Jesus. The more seriously you take your religion, the more liable you are to fall into the trap of Pharisaism. I know that it is easy to publicly whip the Pharisees. They lived a long time ago. None of them will get angry if I scold them in the pulpit. But I have not the heart to take that route. Most of us have not the stomach to live by the rigor and the discipline of the Pharisees. Further, I think there is a larger picture that needs to be told. So I want to back up and take the overview today. Rather than just picking at the text, I want to get from it the sense. I want to think about moral progression today.

I. The Way God Rears His Children

The Bible is filled with laws and teachings. Moses gave us the Ten Commandments. Jesus spoke the Sermon on the Mount. The Book of Proverbs is filled with wise sayings. All of these make a compendium, a veritable source book for right living. When someone says, "I try to live by the Bible," you understand the frame of reference being used. I can honestly say, shortcomings not withstanding, that I try to order my life by the Bible.

But to say that you try to live by the Bible does not deal with the problem. What is the Bible trying to do with us? How is God working with us? And more to the point, how is God trying to rear his children? This is what I want to explain in a way you can hear. Let me give you a little diagram that may stick in your mind . . .

(Put on the board three words: paganism, legalism, and grace. Make these words in the form of stairsteps. Paganism will be at the bottom. Legalism in the middle. Grace will be at the top of the ascending stair of words.)

1. Paganism. Untamed. Savage. Primitive. These are the words that have been used to describe our original condition. Left in our first state, we would be "me first" people. The veneer of culture and civilization would quickly fall away. We would be little more than educated savages. In fact, education may have nothing to do with morality. Nazi Germany is a case in point. A very educated people performed gross sins. Karl Barth asked, "Which is a better mark for mankind, a good man on a horse or a bad man in an airplane?"

All of this has a theological dimension. In Genesis we are told that God put the human family out of the Garden of Eden. We had sinned. We had asserted ourselves against the rule of God. Pride, appetites, and temptation—each had done its part. The human family was fallen. Whether in history we read of the meanness of the Spaniards raping the Aztec, whether in *The Lord of the Flies* literature calls us to remember our fallenness, or whether a psychologist unravels the schemings of the self-willed—all tell the old Bible story. We are pagan. We are fallen. And the good news in our Bible is that God is not content that we should stay in so depraved a state. God has moved to save us.

2. <u>Legalism</u>. God's great effort with the people of Israel was through Moses. Moses went into Egypt, found the slaves, and set about to gain their release. But it was not just into the wilderness these slaves went; it was to the sacred mountain. We know that mountain as Sinai. There God gave to the people a law. The law was long, and the law was sealed with a covenant, but we call that law the Ten Commandments. If the people were to do God's work in the world, they were to live by God's rules.

The rules were much more than just the Ten Commandments. How do you get your sins forgiven? How do you treat a neighbor who does you wrong? What do you do if you get sick? How do you treat your wife? How are you to rear your children? What are you to do with the stranger who comes into your land? How do you worship? Who is to lead worship? And on and on the list goes. You can find these rules listed in the Old Testament. Moses said these rules were from God and that the people were to obey them. And though there was faith in the Old Testament, for the common people there was a set of rules. Do right, and you would be accepted of God.

The apostle Paul referred to the law as a "schoolmaster" (Gal. 3:24-25). Here is the way the *Good News Bible* says it: "So the Law was in charge of us until Christ came, in order that we might then be put right with God through faith. Now that the time for faith is here, the Law is no longer in charge of us" (Gal. 3:24-25, GNB). Note that legalism is a step in the process. It is an upward step, but it is not the end of the process. God gave the law just as God gave us grace in Jesus Christ. But the law was not meant to be the end of the journey.

3. <u>Grace</u>. Finally, in "the fulness of the time," Jesus came (Gal. 4:4). It was toward grace and by grace that God had been leading his children all along. Grace is the reconciliation with God that has been needed since Eden's damage. It is through faith in Christ that God has changed us. We are no longer God's enemies; now we are God's friends (see 2 Cor. 5:18-19). The One we feared, we now want to be

close to. The One we fled, we now run toward. The One we could scarcely take in is now at least understood in part thanks to the Word made flesh (see John 1:14). Because of grace, we see God through the eyes of one who looks at Jesus.

There is a qualitative difference in legalism and grace. In legalism, we must do our religion. It is the doing that commends us to God. But in grace all is gift. God has given his own dear Son, the Good One for the bad ones. The apostle Paul would put it this way: "When we were still helpless, Christ died for the wicked . . . It is a difficult thing for someone to die for a righteous person. . . . But God has shown us how much he loves us—it was while we were still sinners that Christ died for us!" (Rom. 5:6-8, GNB). This means that we did not earn our salvation. It is gift. God has given it. In fact, Jesus is described as God's Gift (see John 3:16). Though there is little change in the outward style of a legalist and one who lives under grace, the underlying presuppositions of legalism and grace are light years apart. The one has earned his place with God. The other has been given place with God. The one is inclined to boast; the other knows that it is all a gift. God is trying to bring us out of paganism to legalism for a time. But his real intention is to lift us on to grace. That is why Jesus came.

II. The Pitfalls of Child Rearing

The text of the day is one of the pitfalls of child rearing. God is trying to bring us along, but we get tangled up in the moral growth process. Pharisees were so right until they became wrong. Let me see if I can put the Pharisees on the moral map.

(Draw a fourth step. Put it beyond legalism but beneath it and well below grace.)

There are some real hazards in child rearing. Some of us tried hard to rear our children, but several things are interlocking in the process. In the first place, we do not get to move our children about in life as we would move the pieces on a chessboard. They have minds of their own. God has had the same problem. He has tried hard to move some of us. We have proven to have minds of our own, wills so strong that we can even frustrate God's best wishes for us.

But more than self-will, I want to identify a couple of risks in moral development.

1. <u>The Risk of Making Light of Legalism</u>. Often preachers make light of legalism. It is all bad. It is well below the New Testament. It is immoral to be legalistic. This is all partly true. The point I want to make now is that legalism is a step above where most of the world is living. For some of you, life is a mess! It is a long row of cravings and appetites, appetites you have satisfied to the full. You are not a legalist; you have always dreaded legalism. But for you legalism would order your life. It would be a step up for you. Do not make light of legalism. Every drug addict and alcoholic, every gambler and workaholic, every intemperate soul would be saved from the gross if only that one would come up to legalism. Be careful. Legalism is bad only when one is trapped in it. Getting to it is a forward step by God's grace.

2. <u>But Some People Have Gotten to Legalism</u>. They have gotten there with a bang. It has been a big deal for them. Maybe it is a little like running for me. I needed to run. I was helped by running. And I was insufferable in telling all about my running. It was the hope of the world.

Compared to the moral earnestness of most of the people who were around Jesus, the Pharisees were truly orderly, disciplined, God-haunted people. They were the Puritans of their time. If you know Colonial history, you know just how miserable the Puritans made everyone else with their religion. Puritans were right. They would order the land to their perception of God's way. Puritans could use the laws of the state to make people be good. (This idea is still with us.) Of course, Puritans were judgmental, severe, and poor models of forgiveness and grace.

Pharisees sometimes appear in earnest church people. We are taking our religion seriously. We are earnest, moral, straight. But we are hard to be around. We make others uncomfortable; they suspect that we judge them. Our prayers are not so much offered to God as they are testimonials to our own moral rectitude. One cynic said of a Puritan prayer, it was "the most eloquent prayer ever offered to a Boston audience."[1] Of course, the flaw here is that prayers are not to be offered to audiences but to God, and it is right here that the text bites. The Pharisee's prayer commended himself to God; his virtues were recited. Finally, he put it all on the line: "I thank you that I am not like that tax collector over there" (Luke 18:11, GNB). This man's moral yardstick was his neighbor. Such are the sins of legalism when made the final point in the moral journey.

III. The Rules to Keep Us Straight

All the stories of Jesus point to rules to guide us. Three of these rules are in this story. If these rules are honored, they will keep us on track, keep us from getting trapped in legalism for a lifetime.

1. Pride Destroys Our Perception. For all of the Pharisee's dedication, still the Pharisee becomes a tragic figure. He kept the rules for so long that he came to think he had commended himself to God. God had not given him salvation; he had earned it. So the Pharisee's prayer is filled with a glowing estimate of himself. "I thank you, God, that I am not greedy, dishonest, or an adulterer, like everybody else" (Luke 18:11, GNB). But keeping external rules does not amend our inward state, and sin is a matter of the heart.

I recall the time at the Fat Stock Show in Fort Worth when I first stood in front of the mirror that made me look ten feet tall and six inches wide. It was some distortion of my real appearance! Pride makes us to think more of ourselves than we ought. Pride makes worship impossible. We do not need God; we are god!

2. An Awareness of Sin Makes Worship Possible. The tax collector had no illusions about his moral condition. Whatever others thought of him, he knew he was sinful. This sure knowledge of need was the precondition that made forgiveness and God's grace possible. So while the rules-keeping man came to the Temple to tell God of his goodness, the sinner came to worship with no thought other than God. "God, have pity on me, a sinner!" is a good posture to begin any worship service (Luke 18:13, GNB). This is the frame of mind that opens the door to reconciliation.

3. God Is the Ultimate Moral Yardstick. This rule is crucial. If we come to church comparing ourselves to everyone else in the house, we have surely set in motion self-justification. Sometimes some of

you with a twinkle in your eye have gone out the back door saying, "You surely told 'em today." You are aware of what you are saying. You know that any word from God was not meant for "them"; it was meant for us, all of us.

I could make myself to look big if I should call Hunter Herring to come up and stand beside me. But that comparison would not last long. If Hunter's father came and stood beside me, I would be the dwarfed one. Such is equally true in the moral arena. One is good when compared to another.

William Barclay, in commenting on this story, told of an incident that happened on one of his journeys. He took the train from Glasgow to London. While riding south across the Yorkshire moors his eye fell upon a lovely, white cottage. It was shining brightly in the sun and looked so clean and white. A few days later he was on his homeward journey. A lovely snow had fallen. Soon the white cottage came into view. But in contrast to the snow, the clean cottage looked "drab and soiled and almost grey—in comparison with the virgin whiteness of the driven snow."[2] The Pharisee compared himself to the tax collector; the tax collector compared himself to the living God. All of us fall short when we measure ourselves by the words and life of Jesus. Jesus is our best insight into the holiness of God.

Conclusion

Moral progression is what God is about. He wants to save us from paganism. To do this he leads us into legalism. But legalism is not the end of the journey. In fact, if we stop there, we have aborted God's intention. The Pharisee's sin was that he stopped short of what God had in mind for him. Go on. Move on up. God has sent his Son, and all who give themselves into his care are given grace. This is where God has been leading us all along. Move on up. Step up to grace. It is amazing but true: the last step is not earned; it is for those who can accept the gift.

Notes

1. William Barclay, *The Gospel of Luke* (Edinburgh: The Saint Andrew Press, 1953), p. 232.

2. Ibid., p. 234.

6

Legitimate Shortcuts in Sermon Preparation

Lavonn D. Brown

I have tried not to be too introspective as to why I was assigned this topic. In fact, I was rather excited about it until I noticed the severely limiting word <u>legitimate</u>. That would give most ministers pause. Regardless, we now leave the world of theory and take up the very practical matter of shortcuts to sermon preparation.

Any preacher who preaches as many as three times a week, week after week, month after month, year after year, will use shortcuts. Some of these will be legitimate, some not so legitimate. The conscientious minister is constantly searching for the legitimate.

Most ministers are aware of the not-so-legitimate approaches, even though they may feel compelled at times to use them. Some ministers will use another's sermon outright. This is the attitude, "When better sermons are written, I'll preach them." Others will use the <u>Saturday Night Special</u> approach which has its historical counterparts dating back to the Middle Ages. Mail-order weekly sermon outlines are popular with some. Another popular approach is the move-every-three-years-and-start-again theory.

The question every minister faces is, Where are we to find a consistent supply of worthy sermon ideas? Must we awaken in a new world every Monday morning? Is there any continuity to what we are doing? Are there legitimate shortcuts to our sermon preparation? The answer is in the affirmative. Let's consider a few.

Beginning with the Text and/or Idea Provided

The minister spends much of his time in the search for texts and ideas. This problem consumes even more of his time when there is

106

no planning, no movement, no progression, and no building on previously laid foundations.

However, most ministers become aware along the way of readily available sources for preaching texts and/or ideas. Some of these are quite legitimate.

Preaching from the Lectionary.—I am not sure when the lectionary fell into disfavor with evangelicals. All I know is that I had never heard of it until recent years. Perhaps I had been told but did not have "ears to hear."

The lectionary provides carefully selected Old and New Testament passages for each Sunday of the year. It is based on a three year cycle—years A, B, and C. Its purpose is to unfold the full sweep of God's revelation. It is a time-tested antidote for the subjectivism which plagues our pulpits. One who follows its suggested readings is preaching out of the wholeness that belongs to the history of the church.

The prayer books of liturgical churches follow the lectionary. Some ministers manuals published annually will also follow the lectionary readings. One volume and multivolume sets are published regularly to give homiletical help based on the common lectionary lessons.[1]

I am not suggesting that the minister become a slave to suggested ideas or texts. This approach may become too rigid and may destroy creativity. However, I am suggesting that the conscientious minister, in his search for ideas, may not wish to ignore this source of carefully selected Scripture readings for each Sunday of the year.

Preaching from the Church Year or Christian Calendar.—Generally speaking, Southern Baptists have been more aware of the traditional Christian year than of the lectionary. They are closely related. Certainly the lectionary will not ignore the major celebrations of the church year. However, the minister may use the Christian calendar to influence his preaching ministry from Sunday to Sunday without slavishly following the lectionary readings for each Sunday of the year.

The purpose and limitations of this article will not permit a full discussion of the rich and limitless resources of the Christian calendar. The minister who wishes to study it more fully should consider J. Winston Pearce's *Planning Your Preaching.* He gives three chapters to a development of what he calls "The Garment of Celebration," a preaching plan based on the Christian year.[2]

Pearce shows that the Christian year is divided into two main sections of approximately equal length. The Lord's half year begins with Advent and concludes with either Pentecost or Trinity Sunday. It includes Christmas, Epiphany, Lent, Easter, and Ascension Day. The church's half year begins with Pentecost or Trinity Sunday and runs to the beginning of the Advent season. Since it contains none of the major times of celebration, this half year emphasizes Christian instruction, growth, and initiative.

The key is completeness. The Christian year provides a framework within which the full gospel may be approached. It does so by majoring on seven great seasons: Advent, Christmas, Epiphany, Lent, Easter, Pentecost, Trinity (and/or Kingdomtide).

The greatest value of the Christian year for the evangelical minister is in its seasonal suggestions. The minister in search for ideas will find strong possibilities in the winter and spring celebrations (Christmas and Easter) on the Christian calendar. Both of these special occasions deserve adequate preparation.

For instance, the Advent season provides four Sundays for the celebration of Christmas. The word Advent means "coming" or "arrival." It begins on the Sunday closest to November 30 and lasts for four Sundays. Each Sunday has its own special emphasis. The perceptive minister will use all four of these Sundays as a season of preparation for the coming of Christ. One Christmas sermon on the Sunday prior to December 25 is hardly adequate preparation.

The celebration of Christian resurrection on Easter also deserves adequate preparation. The minister may wish to "back up" on his calendar from Easter Sunday and prepare a series of sermons that will climax on that day. This would be an excellent time to preach a series on the "Crises in the life of Christ." Such a series should include sermons on his baptism, temptations, transfiguration, crucifixion, resurrection (on Easter), and ascension. Once again, this provides for adequate preparation for a major celebration on the

Christian calendar. The church must be prepared for celebrating great religious festivals in the same way they must be prepared for revival.

The conscientious minister, constantly searching for sermon ideas, must not ignore or fear the resources available from an awareness of the church year or Christian calendar.

Preaching Biblical Series on Sunday Evenings.—Most Southern Baptist pastors preach at least twice on Sundays. This means they must discover twice as many ideas or texts as ministers of other denominations. Some ministers have discovered that preaching biblical series on Sunday evenings relieves part of the pressure. The dedicated people who return for the Sunday evening service will respond with gratitude to this direct approach to Bible study. The possibilities are unlimited. Each minister will approach this challenge in a way pleasing to his own nature and personality.

Chalmer Faw, in his book *A Guide to Biblical Preaching*, describes a program of preaching that moves from larger to smaller portions of Scripture.[3] This one approach would provide ideas and texts for Sunday evening series for many years. The minister is free to use all or any part of his suggested approach.

This gradation approach would begin with the largest possible passage of Scripture, one sermon on the Bible as a whole. Preaching one 25-minute sermon on the entire Bible is a good discipline. The next logical divisions would be one sermon each on both the Old and New Testament.

Next comes the sixty-six books of the Bible. One sermon based on each of the books of the Bible is of benefit both to the preacher and the hearer. The minister may wish to follow a "Book of the Month" approach, introducing his people to a new book of the Bible each month.

Continuing the movement from larger to smaller units of Scripture, some books of the Bible may be preached chapter by chapter (Acts, Amos, Jonah, Hosea). Others lend themselves more to a paragraph by paragraph approach (John, Luke, Ephesians, James, 1 John, Philippians).

While doing the study for the above sermons, endless ideas for briefer series on shorter texts will present themselves. The Sermon on the Mount (Matthew 5—7) and the Ten Commandments may be approached in a verse by verse study. Briefer series on great chapters, great personalities, the parables of Jesus, and so forth are available for Sunday evening preaching.

The minister who carefully considers the lectionary, the Christian year, and biblical series should suffer from an embarrassment of riches where sermon ideas and texts are concerned.

Beginning with a Potential Outline for the Sermon

Often the minister spends much of his time attempting to give unity and movement to his sermon. Some kind of outline or structure is essential in bringing order out of chaos. This structure may be obvious only to the preacher, but it is essential nonetheless.

Over the years the preacher will become increasingly aware of readily available approaches to outlining which are quite legitimate. The minister may even begin with an outline in mind, changing from it only if a better approach is discovered. Each person must develop potential outlines which fits his own style.

I will suggest a few approaches that are commonly used. None is sacred.

When Dealing with a Text.—Unity and movement may be achieved by using what are commonly known as the functional elements of preaching. A basic outline may come from three major steps toward the completed sermon: interpretation, illustration, and application.

The first step toward the completed sermon (and potentially the first major division of the outline) is interpretation or explanation. Here the text is explained, made clear, made understandable. At this point it must be said that there is no legitimate shortcut to take the place of the minister's own personal study of the text. Each preacher must know the steps to proper exegesis. He must come to his own understanding of the text. He must discover for himself the central idea of the passage. More than anything else, this distinguishes one man's sermons from another's.

The second step toward the completed sermon (and potentially the second major division of the outline) is illustration. The purpose of the illustration is to make clear, picture, throw light on the central truth of the sermon. Illustrations are essential to communication in our picture conscious age. However, most ministers choose to incorporate illustrations into other parts of the sermon, rather than giving them the status of a major division. Regardless, outlining is made more simple when the minister is aware that illustration is one of the steps toward the completed sermon.

The third step toward the completed sermon (and potentially the third major division of the outline) is application. Here the central truth is related directly to the congregation. The hearer is involved and moved toward positive action. The questions here are, Where does God encounter the human situation in this text? What is God attempting to say to you and me in this passage?

In the course of study, another outline or structure may present itself to the minister. In that case, these functional elements may still be used to fill in the major divisions selected. Interpretation, illustration, and application will add meat and muscle to the skeleton.

<u>When dealing with a Topic or Life Situation.</u>—The minister will often take a problem-solving approach to preaching. The Bloom Agency made a study of Texas to determine people's most pressing needs. These were to be used in television advertising in preparation for a statewide evangelistic effort. They found that the "ten most pressing needs" of people were: alienation, fear of death, inner emptiness, family turmoil, purposelessness, hopelessness, loneliness, peace of mind, guilt, and lack of self-control.

The most popular approach to outlining these life-situation sermons is simply to identify the causes and cures, or the problem and solution. What are the factors contributing to this problem? What does the Bible have to say that will help?

In such cases, the preacher begins his study with a potential outline in mind and will use it unless he discovers something better in the process.

<u>Other Functional Outlines to Consider.</u>—The two point outline mentioned above has appeared in many forms. The minister should

be a collector of functional outlines for possible use. Some examples are: comparison—contrast, problem—solution, negative—positive, divine—human, time—eternity.

A new emphasis is now being placed on "story preaching." The word story is used to mean narration. This approach encourages the preacher to be a good storyteller. It asks, Why can't sermons be stories? After all, the Bible is essentially a storybook. When the sermon becomes shared story, the structure of the sermon is merely the structure of the story.[4]

The minister is placed in a point of great advantage when he has accumulated general outlines that will work when all else fails. In this way, he begins with an outline in mind but may change from it if a better approach is discovered. This is certainly a legitimate approach to sermon preparation.

Reworking Worthy Ideas from the Past

I suppose every minister has struggled with the reuse of past materials. We have in our files sermons that are worthy, biblical, and have blessed past congregations. Should they be used again?

W. E. Sangster in *The Craft of the Sermon* says, "Some men think it is dishonoring to God not to prepare a new sermon every time they mount the pulpit steps, but that is a rule I find unconvincing."[5]

Worthy ideas from the past not only may be repeated, but often people will request that a sermon be given again. There are times when this is a legitimate shortcut to sermon preparation. What should be the preacher's considerations in reworking and reusing these materials?

First, he should allow sufficient time to pass. This, of course, will vary from sermon to sermon. Some have suggested that sermons may be repeated after only a few months if you change the illustrations. Obviously, a sermon built on one classic, memorable illustration should not be soon repeated. Being in a university setting, my personal practice is to avoid repeating a sermon within a student generation (four years). The only exceptions being requested sermons, seasonal sermons, or sermon ideas completely reworked.

69165

Second, the preacher should make the idea glow again. Sangster warned, "Don't repeat your own sermons unless you can glow over them."[6] Obviously, the preacher should not go on repeating a sermon when it has secretly ceased to thrill his own heart and fails to kindle within him as the word of God should.

The idea should be reworked. The argument should be re-thought. The relevance of the idea should be questioned. The old wine should be put in new wine skins. Surely the preacher has learned something new of life and of God since the sermon was last preached.

A third consideration is that new, fresh, current illustrations should be used. Old, timeworn illustrations are remembered first. The minister should continue his search for illustrations for sermons already preached. A filing system must be developed that makes it possible to add new materials to work already done.

Finally, there are legitimate plans for repeating sermons in series form. Some ministers set aside a time on the calendar for a "preach it again" series. Generally the summer months are used for this. Others will keep a list of "sermons you have asked for" and offer them in a summer series.

My own practice is to use the summer months for reading and for the preparation of a preaching calendar for the next nine months. I prepare very few new sermons during the summer. I go back to the sermons prepared four years earlier and repeat eight to twelve of them during summer. I tend to select life-situational, problem-solving themes for these difficult summer Sundays.

The Legitimate Use of Another's Idea

Here we must deal with a problem that has no ultimate solution. It is as widely practiced as it is consistently denied. Is it ever legitimate to use outright another's material? is the question.

Some ministers seem to do this with no pangs of conscience. Of course, the threshold of pain differs from minister to minister where the conscience is concerned. Some struggle with unbelievable guilt at this point; others do not. The answer must be somewhere in between the two extremes.

Plagiarism involves the use of another's message as though it were your own. The word literally means "kidnapper" or "abductor." Apparently, the practice was not considered a problem until after the Reformation. Prior to that, according to one church historian, the practice of appropriating materials wholesale and without credit "was not disapproved when it was done with skill, and when the ideas and words taken from another were used with success."[7]

A. W. Blackwood in *The Preparation of Sermons* makes reference to books of sermons entitled *Sleep Well Sermons* published during the Middle Ages in Europe.[8] They became so popular among parish priests that they passed through twenty-five editions. He was careful to point out that the title "Sleep Without Care" referred to the priests and not to the hearers. The idea was that the priest could busy himself with other matters and then sleep well on Saturday night. This was the historical counterpart to "The Saturday Night Special."

Even though this practice fell into disrepute in more recent years, religious book store managers continue to report that most clergymen seem to rely heavily on the printed sermons and the outlines of other ministers. In recent times, this problem has become even more complicated because laypeople are also buying the books. It is not uncommon for a layperson to have in hand the book his pastor is using for a series of sermons.

For many reasons, it is best for the minister when preaching a sermon not his own to frankly admit it. The same would be true of a striking, memorable outline. The preacher is clearly no plagiarist who takes a sermon and tells his congregation from whose sermons it was taken. Nor is he a plagiarist when he seeks stimulation for his mind by reading the sermons of others. The minister may take the milk of others but should churn his own butter. Or as Sangster put it, "To cut a piece of cloth off another man's roll is not, I think, a sin in literature of homiletics, but to steal the suit that he has made and parade it as one's own is plain theft."[9]

Whatever the minister does in this regard should be kept proper or appropriate. There must be proper limitations placed on the use of another's materials. For instance, the preacher must develop ways of giving credit to those who have made a major contribution to his thoughts. He might say "I wish I could take credit for the ideas I share with you today. The truth is a minister friend saw these truths in this text long before I."

Blackwood has suggested that the minister should submit his plans to the "test of publicity."[10] How would you handle the situation if the person who wrote the sermon were present in your congregation?

Legitimate Worship Experiences that
May not Include the Sermon

Most pastors will want to protect the Sunday morning worship service for preaching. This is to be expected and encouraged. However, in many churches (especially Southern Baptist), there may be as many as two other worship services where preaching is a possibility.

The Wednesday evening prayer service is considered by many a "preaching" service. Others have changed the nature of these weekly services to include meaningful prayer experiences, testimony services, and perhaps the giving of a brief devotional idea. This is a legitimate approach to worship that does not require the preparation of a "full-blown" sermon.

The Sunday evening services provide endless possibilities for a variety of forms of worship. This is especially true in the larger church where the pastor has other trained professional people on his staff helping him plan for worship. Even though the Sunday evening service should probably retain its primary character as a preaching service, the pastor may consider from time to time legitimate alternatives to the sermon.[11]

Some alternatives will still require preparation for the worship experience but not sermon preparation. One example would be a Sunday evening service given to the observance of the ordinances, baptism and the Lord's Supper.[12] The dramatic monologue and the dialogue sermon also require preparation even though another's materials might be used. The minister may wish to use the Sunday evening service at the close of Christian Home Week for a Christian wedding ceremony.

Other legitimate alternatives to the sermon would require less preparation on the preacher's part: drama, motion pictures, multimedia presentations, panel discussion, interviews, concerts, sermons in song, and planned testimony services. However, these services often require preparation on the part of others.

Conclusion

In the beginning, I stated that any preacher who preaches as many as three times a week, week after week, month after month, year after year, will use shortcuts. Some of these will be legitimate, some not so legitimate.

Most ministers are aware of the not-so-legitimate approaches. The purpose of this paper has been to present some legitimate approaches. If the result eases the load for a fellow minister, then my time and effort have been well spent.

NOTES

1. Reginald Fuller, *Preaching the New Lectionary* (Collegeville: The Liturgical Press, 1974), pp. 1-530.

2. J. Winston Pearce, *Planning Your Preaching* (Broadman Press, Nashville, 1967), chs. 3—5.

3. Chalmer Faw, *A Guide to Biblical Preaching* (Broadman Press, Nashville, 1962).

4. Steimle, Niedenthal, and Rice, *Preaching the Story* (Fortress Press, Philadelphia, 1980). Richard A. Jensen, *Telling the Story* (Augsburg Publishing, Minneapolis, 1980).

5. W. E. Sangster, *The Craft of the Sermon* (Westminster Press, Philadelphia, 1950), p. 201.

6. Ibid., p. 201.

7. Wm. M. Ramsay, *St. Paul, The Traveller and the Roman Citizen* (G. P. Putnam's Sons, New York, 1901), p. 242. Andrew W. Blackwood, *The Preparation of Sermons* (Abingdon-Cokesbury Press, 1948), p. 243.

8. Ibid., pp. 243-244. E. C. Dargan, *A History of Preaching* (A. C. Armstrong & Sons, New York, 1905), I, pp. 187, 309.

9. W. E. Sangster, p. 200.

10. Andrew Blackwood, p. 249.

11. Robert W. Bailey, *New Ways in Christian Worship* (Broadman Press, Nashville, 1981).

12. James C. Barry and Jack Gulledge, *Ideas for Effective Worship Services* (Convention Press, Nashville, 1977), p. 59-60.

Bloom Where You're Planted
Genesis 45:1-15

(This particular sermon was selected for a number of reasons. It illustrates one method of "telling the story" or narrative-style preaching. It is also an example of how a longer text might be used, since it covers ten chapters in Genesis. The structure is simple and does not require great imagination. Since the sermon simply presents scenes or episodes in the life of Joseph, unity and movement come from the story itself.)

Most people live out their lives waiting on something to happen to make them happy. Always sure that happiness is just around the corner, they wait for someone to show up, some circumstance to change, some situation to develop. They are waiting on a job promotion, a divorce, a marriage situation to improve, children to grow up, or a change in location. Then they will be happy.

A part of what it means to be made in "the image of God" is that we are given freedom of will and choice (Gen. 1:27). It means that in every given situation, we do have an alternative. We are not always free to choose what happens to us, but we are free to determine our response. The choice is always ours. We are responsible.

This morning I want to tell you about a man with an amazing gift to be happy under the present circumstances. He was able to "bloom where he was planted." He was forever rising above adverse circumstances, while serving faithfully in favorable circumstances. His name was Joseph. It is a familiar, charming story.

Scene One: Joseph, a Son in Jacob's House (Gen. 37)
Joseph was Jacob's favorite. He was more like a grandson than a

son. Apparently he got too much attention and was sheltered, spoiled, preferred over his brothers, privileged, and somewhat arrogant.

And he was a dreamer. Somehow he always achieved a position of honor in his dreams. Rather than keeping this to himself, he freely told his brothers. They were jealous and resentful. These unblessed sons watched for an opportunity to unseat their father's pet. Their time came.

Joseph was sent by his father to check on the welfare of his brothers who were tending sheep. When he arrived, they tossed him into a well. We look down into the well and say, "Welcome to the real world, Joseph."

Later, they decided to sell Joseph to a band of traveling traders. He was carried off into Egypt, away from Palestine forever. For all he knew, he would live the rest of his life as a slave in a foreign land.

Scene Two: Joseph, a Slave in Potiphar's House (Gen. 39)

Now Joseph is far away from family, friends, and homeland. He is a slave in Potiphar's house. Potiphar is the captain of the guard, an officer of the Egyptian pharaoh. How will Joseph react to his new situation?

Psychiatrists tell us that the two normal reactions would be fight or flight. Joseph could have struggled against his circumstances, cursed his brothers, and lived with resentment. As a slave he could have done as little as possible and certainly only what was demanded. Or he could have watched for every opportunity to escape and lived for some future day when he would be free. But what did he do?

He was not free to choose his circumstances; he was free to choose his response. The choice was his. He chose to "bloom where he was planted." He worked hard. He was clean and honest, decent and bright. His religious background gave him a basic trustworthiness. He worked his way up through the ranks until he became Potiphar's chief butler. Potiphar made Joseph overseer of his house and "left all that he had in Joseph's charge" (Gen. 39:6, RSV).

Then came the episode with Potiphar's wife. It is the age-old story of the bored housewife and the handsome, young Hebrew slave. Her husband was seldom home and constantly busy. Taking advantage of a time when her husband was away, she tried to seduce Joseph. Once again, the choice was his. He refused. Potiphar's wife was insulted and furious. Joseph was falsely accused and sent to the royal prison where he was thrown into a dungeon.

Scene Three: Joseph, an Inmate in an Egyptian Prison (Gen. 39)

I should think it would be bad enough being in jail for doing something wrong, but Joseph was falsely accused. He was in prison because he did the right thing. What would he do? How would he respond to his new circumstances?

He could have reacted with bitterness, asking, "Is this the reward for righteousness?" He could have allowed resentment to grow. He could have spent his time studying how to get revenge on Potiphar's wife. Or he could have watched for every opportunity to escape, lived for some future time when he would be free.

Again, he was not free to choose his circumstances; he was free to choose his response. The choice was his. He chose to "bloom where he was planted." He worked hard and proved that he was dependable and trustworthy. He worked his way up through the ranks until "the keeper [warden] of the prison committed to Joseph's care all the prisoners . . . and whatever was done there, he was the doer of it; the keeper of the prison paid no heed to anything that was in Joseph's care" (Gen. 39:22-23, RSV).

In due time the chief butler and the chief baker of the pharaoh became prisoners. Joseph interpreted some dreams for them. One was set free and restored to the pharaoh's favor. Joseph asked to be remembered for his kindness.

Two years later, Pharaoh himself was troubled by a dream. In his dream he was standing by the Nile. Seven fat, healthy cows came up out of the Nile and fed on the grass. Seven thin, sickly cows came up out of the Nile and ate the seven fat cows. The pharaoh's wise men could not interpret his dream (Gen. 41:1-8).

All of a sudden (after two years), the chief butler remembered Joseph in prison. He said, "I had a strange experience in prison. I had a dream. A Hebrew named Joseph interpreted it for me. It came out exactly as he said it would."

Pharaoh sent for Joseph. Joseph told him the meaning of his dream. There would be seven years of abundance followed by seven years of famine. Joseph even proposed a solution. He said that granaries should be built to store the surplus grain during the seven years of abundance. And an administrator should be appointed to oversee the process. Pharaoh was impressed.

Scene Four: Joseph, the Prime Minister in Pharaoh's Palace (Gen. 41)

Pharaoh said to Joseph, "You shall be over my house, and all my people shall order themselves as you command; only as regards the throne will I be greater than you. . . . I have set you over all the land of Egypt" (Gen. 41:40-41, RSV). How would Joseph react to this new set of circumstances? With pride, saying, "Finally, I'm getting what I had coming to me all along?" With self-indulgence? Would he use this new situation to insure his own future? Pad his own pocketbook? Would he simply look out for number one? Or would he use his new resources to get revenge on Potiphar's wife? On his brothers?

Joseph was not free to choose his circumstances; he was free to choose his response. The choice was his. He chose to "bloom where he was planted." He worked hard. He carried out the plan he had submitted to Pharaoh. After seven years, "all the earth came to Egypt to Joseph to buy grain" (Gen. 41:57, RSV).

Finally, his brothers came from Canaan. They bowed themselves with faces to the ground before Joseph. Joseph could have said, "Remember those dreams I told you about years ago?" Even if he thought it, he didn't say it. What he did say to his brothers was: "God sent me before you to preserve for you a remnant, . . . So it was not you who sent me here, but God; and he has made me a father to Pharaoh, and lord of all his house and ruler over all the land of Egypt" (Gen. 45:7-8, RSV). A double agenda had been at work in Joseph's life. God had been at work in it all along.

Scene Five: The Twentieth Century, and the Choice Is Ours

It must be said over and over again. We are not free to choose our circumstances; we are free to choose our response. The choice is always ours. How are you responding to "where you are planted"?

Many are fighting all the way. They curse their circumstances. They live with bitterness and resentment. They do only what life demands. They spend most of their energy studying how to get revenge on those who have shortchanged them. One thing is certain, they are not responsible for the circumstances which cause their unhappiness.

Alexandre Dumas in *The Count of Monte Cristo* tells of a man who spent his entire prison sentence plotting revenge. Edmond Dantes, at 19, was plotted against by three men who envied his job and the girl he loved. They caused him to be thrown into prison.

His prison term was spent in planning escape and plotting revenge. Fourteen years later, having learned of buried treasure while in prison, he did escape. He found the treasure and became fabulously wealthy. He set out to take revenge.

Danglers, a wealthy banker, was gradually brought to poverty. Fernand, who could not face the revelations of his past, committed suicide. Villefort, who had come to high office, had his crime brought forth and went raving mad.

We tend to cheer Edmond on in his pursuits. Deep inside there is a basic satisfaction in seeing the three villains "getting what they have coming" to them.

But in the back of our minds, we are haunted by one who responded to prison in a different way. He made every effort to "bloom where he was planted." More than that, we are haunted by another young man of thirty-three years who faced the hatred of those seeking his life and prayed, "Father, forgive them . . . " (Luke 23:34).

Others are running away. Seeking an escape. Living for the future. Looking for love in all the wrong places. Some who do not like the reality of their lives try to escape into a fantasy world of alcohol and drugs. Others are constantly running, on the move from town to town, church to church, place to place, trying to find some ideal set of circumstances—and happiness.

Robert Hastings has beautifully described their search:

Tucked away in our subconscious minds is an idyllic vision. We see ourselves on a long, long trip that almost spans the continent. . . .

But uppermost in our minds is our destination. A certain day and a certain hour and we'll pull in the station with bands playing and flags waving. . . .

However, sooner or later we must realize there's no one station, no one place to arrive once and for all. The true joy of life is the trip. The station is only a dream. It constantly outdistances us. "When we reach the station, that will be it!" we cry. Translated, this means, "When I'm 18, that will be it!" "When I buy a new 450 SL Mercedes Benz, that will be it!" "When I put the last kid through college, that'll be it!" "When I've paid off the mortgage, that'll be it!" "When I win a promotion, that'll be it!" "When I have a nest egg for retirement, that'll be it! And I'll live happily ever after!"

Unfortunately, once we get "it," then "it" disappears. The station somehow hides itself at the end of an endless track. . . .

So stop pacing the aisles and counting the miles . . . Life must be lived as we go along. The station will come soon enough.[1]

However, the happiest people among us are those who are learning to "bloom where they are planted." The choice is yours. You are not free to choose your situation or circumstances. Some are trying to be Christian in hard places. You are free to choose your response.

Is it possible for you to relish this moment? Can you say with the psalmist, "This is the day which the Lord has made;/let us rejoice and be glad in it" (Ps. 118:24)?

Life must be lived as we go along. Corrie ten Boom asks, "What if in God's sight the way is the destination?" New Testament Christians were called "people of the way," not the destination.

What if you are where you're going? What if what you see is what you get? What if the way is the destination? What if life is what you are living, doing now?

I often watch M*A*S*H on television with my teenage son. I recall one episode where Colonel Potter lamented, "I've spent eighteen Christmases away from Mildred [his wife]. It took me fifteen of them to realize I was making myself miserable by wishing I was someplace I wasn't. *If you ain't where you are, you're no place"* (italics mine).

Conclusion

Perhaps we need to go to work doing one thing at a time, living one day at a time. Someone has said that today is often crucified between two thieves: our regret of yesterday and our fear of tomorrow. Today is really all we have. Life must be lived as we go along. This is another way of saying, "Bloom where you're planted!"

Note

1. Condensed from a column by Robert J. Hastings, editor, *Illinois Baptist*, January 2, 1980.

7

Coordinating Preaching with Church Objectives

William E. Hull

I

The problem addressed in this paper is the tendency of preaching to become peripheral to the central tasks of the pastor. Unless the sermon is perceived as an integral part of those leadership responsibilities in which the minister is engaged throughout the week, it may well become a magnificent irrelevancy, admired for its momentary inspirational impact but isolated from the larger strategies by which a church is guided to fulfill its intended destiny. There are at least three reasons preaching often stands apart in solitary splendor from the more mundane aspects of ministry, a position which many of its advocates seem to covet but which, ironically, may prove to be its curse.

First, preaching is the most ancient and enduring function of ministry in the Free Church tradition, having been practiced by giants since the time of the New Testament. Indeed, until the twentieth century, preaching was the acknowledged king of the pastoral disciplines, ruling over this domain without a major rival. Not until after World War II did serious competitors take the field, especially pastoral counseling and church administration. After almost two thousand years of virtual monopoly, preaching is still in the first generation of its coexistence with these major alternative approaches to ministry; therefore, we should not be surprised that it has scarcely begun to be assimilated to them. After all, much of the classic literature on preaching was written long before 1950, and even much of the material being published today by older authors reflects a pre-1950 imperialistic viewpoint.

Second, there are problems with the way in which preaching continues to be taught to impressionable ministerial students, thereby shaping attitudes that may last for a lifetime. In most seminaries, homiletics has been forced to make room for a host of other "practical" disciplines. Indeed, in some theological schools where homiletics was the largest or only department in "pastoralia" just one generation ago, it is today one of the smaller departments in that division of study. In many cases, this ground has been given grudgingly, at times resulting in a not always friendly competition which denigrates the other pastoral disciplines simply by ignoring them. Several standard textbooks in homiletics seem to imply that preaching is the only thing a pastor has to do! The chief reason for a restricted viewpoint, however, is not professional jealousy toward competing disciplines. Rather, it is rooted in the simple fact that the only thing professors of preaching teach, year after year, is— preaching! This narrow specialization, more than anything else, accounts for the tendency to define homiletics in isolationist fashion, a definition which many students accept before they have the experiential basis to know better.

Third, when a pastor is forced by the exigencies of parish practice to attempt an integration of his segregated seminary curriculum, he encounters a certain conflict of role models in making the effort. Lurking behind his image of preaching is a flaming prophet, behind his image of counseling a cool therapist, behind his image of administration a driving business executive. One wears camel's hair and leather girdle; another wears a long white coat; while yet another wears a three-piece, pinstripe suit. What we have here is a clash of life-styles: the métier of preaching is charismatic, of counseling is clinical, of administration is consultative. The first depends on inspiration, the second on insight, and the third on institutions to achieve its goals. The point is that these differing temperaments and techniques tend to harden into competing personality types which are viewed as mutually incompatible by the young pastor choosing his career patterns.

Surveying this situation from "the trenches," the obvious response is that the practitioner of parish ministry simply does not have the luxury of choosing among these competing options. Unlike the theological professor, he cannot specialize in one discipline or in the life-style which it implies. The working pastor is better served by a unified approach to his task that melds every legitimate method into a holistic pattern of practice possessing integrity, comprehensiveness, and balance. This understanding of ministry will not be achieved, as is so often attempted, by asserting the supremacy of preaching over every other pastoral function. What is needed is not to establish the primacy of preaching over, but rather the unity of preaching with, all of the other essential tasks which the pastor must perform equally well. What we are seeking to magnify here, in other words, is not the centrality of preaching but the centrality of ministry in which preaching occupies its rightful place. How may this be done?

II

The place to start is with a biblically based understanding of preaching. From a scriptural standpoint, preaching is profoundly connected with the people of God. In its divine aspect, a sermon is the voice of God calling the church into being; in its human aspect, it is the voice of the church speaking out of that new being. Stated starkly: no church, no pulpit. This means that the purposes of preaching should parallel the purposes of the people of God. The primary task of the pulpit is to help the church "become what it is." The sermon beckons and propels the people of God toward the fulfillment of their mission here on earth.

This definition determines the agenda for preaching, which is nothing other than everything involved in being/becoming the church in the world. Before spelling out just what that might entail, let me make a strong plea for doing ministry by agenda. Pastoral work exposes a person to an avalanche of urgent claims, both personal and institutional, all of them worthy of immediate attention. The minister who simply responds to whatever comes up next

will always be both busy and useful, but he may never get around to
some things that need doing even more. An agenda shifts one's
leadership style from reactive to proactive. It provides a "table of
contents" by which to organize one's time. In the midst of unavoida-
ble pressures that threaten to overwhelm the decision-making
process, it offers a checklist by which to take stock, a game plan to
make sure that all the bases are being touched. A carefully
conceived agenda is the antidote to normless existence. It is like a
template that can be superimposed over a typical slice of church life
at any time to evaluate its adequacy. The need for agenda is based on
the axiom that if you don't know where you are going, you probably
won't get there!

Those who have followed me to this point will realize that I am
suggesting the use of management by objectives (MBO) in the
exercise of pastoral leadership. This is basically a systems approach
to meeting the needs of an organization by defining its overall
purposes and priorities, then providing the resources and guiding
the processes needed to reach those goals within an acceptable time
frame. In brief, I am adapting this secular model for church use by
deriving its objectives from biblical norms, by defining management
in terms of a servant ministry, and by depending upon the Holy
Spirit to supply the power which congregations need to fulfill their
scriptural mandate.

One reason why MBO is so useful in meeting the problem raised
by this paper is that it permits an effective correlation between
preaching and all of the other tasks of pastoral ministry. Consistent
with what has already been said about the nature of preaching, we
may view the sermon as a means of "managing" (that is, leading) the
church to accomplish its biblical objectives. In other words, into a
comprehensive theory of leadership called "management by objectives," we may fit a compatible theory of homiletics called "preaching by objectives." Rather than standing in isolation or in competition, these two approaches may be viewed as integral parts of what is
sometimes described as an "intentional ministry."

With the problems defined and the theoretical underpinnings of a solution in place, let us move now to design a working model implied by this conceptual framework.

III

I have suggested that the purpose of preaching, indeed of all ministry, is to enable the church to be/become what God intends for the people of God as defined by the biblical revelation and enriched by the continuing guidance of the Holy Spirit. If that be true, then the most crucial agenda for any preacher to construct is that which the New Testament church set for itself. Based on my study of the primary sources, I find six "marks" which are essential if the church is to be/become itself in every age (see Acts 2:41-47).

(1) Worship. The gathering of the "congrega-tion" as a demonstration of its essential solidarity, a visible realm where reconciliation has been realized through the unity of the Spirit. The proclamation of the Word and the celebration of the divine Presence as the energizing of the body to experience renewal through the judgment and mercy of God. The anticipation of the world to come which both nourishes the holiness of the people of God and empowers them for service in the present age.

(2) Outreach. The guiding of persons to God through the saving work of Jesus Christ. The forthright declaration of the message of salvation with a compassionate invitation to accept its offer of new life through repentance and faith. The evangelizing of all who profess no personal relationship to Jesus Christ and the enlisting of unaffiliated Christians who need a vital connection with the family of faith.

(3) Nurture. The developing of believers into mature disciples through a study of the Scriptures, training in doctrine and ethics, and enrichment through such participatory activities as music and recreation. The growth of the inner spiritual life, the strengthening of family and vocational ties, and the edifying of the congregation by the discovery and training of those with gifts for leadership.

(4) Fellowship. The undergirding of believers in such struggles as

the temptation to sin, the danger of backsliding, the ravages of disease, and the hurt of bereavement. The offering of encouragement and counsel in such crises of life as marriage, childbirth, retirement, and death. The sharing of a common life in bonds of mutual love.

(5) Service. The prophetic role of the church in the world, challenging evils entrenched in the collective structures of society, liberating the oppressed from exploitation, seeking to build a more just and humane world in which to live. The servant role of the church in the world, extending benevolence to the unfortunate, encouragement to the victims of exploitation, and rehabilitation to those who seek to overcome a legacy of failure. The apostolic role of the church in the world, working directly and cooperatively to extend the gospel throughout the earth.

(6) Support. The allocation and administration of all the human and material resources of the church to facilitate the effective implementation of its essential ministries.

If these six dimensions characterize an authentic New Testament church wherever it may be found, then the primary agenda of any ministry should be to help a congregation express each of these facets in its contemporary life. Every management function would then be approached in terms of these six objectives (which may be particularized in given times and places):

(1) To conduct regular services of worship which express the unity of the members in one body, which lay the claims of the Christian faith upon every hearer of the Word, and which provide an experience of the presence and power of the triune God to all who believe.

(2) To seek out all persons responsive to the ministry of our church and encourage their acceptance of the saving message of Jesus Christ expressed through personal commitment to his lordship and active involvement as a member of our fellowship.

(3) To guide a process of Christian growth toward mature discipleship through experiences of study, training, and sharing that will enrich each member in all relationships of life and thereby build up the body of Christ into the likeness of its Head.

(4) To guard the flock from threats to its well-being by sustaining members in times of difficulty and encouraging them in times of opportunity through a caring fellowship equipped to bear one another's burdens.

(5) To meet the deepest needs of humanity through worldwide missionary and benevolent service that combats those forces which thwart the intention of God for each individual and for society.

(6) To provide the administrative support needed for the effective fulfillment of all other ministries of the church indicated above.

Before moving to our primary concern with preaching, let me first indicate how I seek to fulfill my management responsibilities as a minister in accordance with these six objectives of our church. I only regret that there is not space to illustrate these applications in greater detail.

(1) The First Baptist Church in Shreveport currently sponsors twenty-six continuing programs of ministry, all of which are organized into six comprehensive "ministry systems" defined by the above objectives. All weekly, monthly, and annual staff reports follow this format. All data is collected and conserved in accordance with these categories, whether on computer or in the church files. Quite simply, we as a church think in these terms when doing all of our work.

(2) Regarding staff personnel, all departmental and divisional alignments, as well as all supervisory relationships, follow this sixfold structure. All position descriptions are written to insure that every component in each of the ministry systems is adequately covered in terms of staff assignments. Time management techniques are employed to insure that adequate staff attention is devoted to each phase of ministry.

(3) Fiscal management: program budgeting is used to identify the financial resources needed to undergird each ministry system and its component parts. A double chart of accounts permits us to keep track of the various types of expenditures by line items (for example, salaries, benefits, office support) without thereby obscuring the more important issue of the total amount invested annually to achieve each ministry objective. Even the prioritizing and budget-

ing for capital projects are considered within this same framework.

(4) The organizational structure of the lay leadership is also determined by these six objectives. All standing church committees, councils, and boards exist as working groups responsible for the formulation of strategies to accomplish these goals. The decision-making flow involving lay leaders parallels that involving staff leaders so that the efforts of both groups are coordinated at every level. Even reports and recommendations to the Church Conference follow this sixfold framework so that our agenda at that meeting accurately reflects our ongoing agenda for ministry.

I am hopeful that this swift sketch will hint at our efforts to relate every activity, every schedule, every expenditure, and every meeting to a coherent agenda for ministry. Which brings us back to the pulpit. One of my chief tasks as pastor is to use the sermon as an instrument for interpreting our biblical mandate to minister and motivating the congregation to accept this challenge in all its fullness. The best way to ensure that I will get this done is to make our church's agenda for ministry the organizing principle for all of my pastoral preaching. Now let me explain in very practical terms how this is done.

IV

There are, of course, many criteria for planning one's pulpit work, and I use most of them to some extent. For example, I take seriously the climactic days both of the Christian year (for example, Christmas, Easter) and of the American year (for example, Independence Day, Thanksgiving Day). I seek balance in preaching from all parts of the Bible and on every type of human need. I am careful to vary my methods, for example, as between textual, expository, and topical approaches. But all such plans, whether taken separately or together, do not add up to a total strategy for pastoral preaching that insures integrity, comprehensiveness, and balance. I have found that the best plan is based on an understanding of preaching as God's call to the church to fulfill its biblical mandate for ministry.

The appendix attached to this paper seeks to set forth in outline form what I consider to be an agenda for preaching rooted in the ministry mandate of the church. Here, in other words, is an approach to preaching by objectives that attempts to extend the management function of pastoral leadership to the pulpit. I invite your scrutiny of that skeletal outline at this point in the present paper.

Perhaps it will help you to grasp just how I use this approach if we walk through the process somewhat in chronological order.

(1) Whenever I get a sermon idea, whether from scriptural study or current reading or personal experience, the first question I ask is what objective that idea will help me to accomplish within my total ministry. Once I grasp that key point, I then jot down both the idea and its possible usage for inclusion in a three-ring notebook with tab guides that correspond to the outline of a preaching agenda described in the appendix. This means that when the time comes to preach on a particular ministry need, such as prayer or evangelism or stewardship, I can find all of my "sermon starters" on that agenda gathered at the same place for ease of selection.

(2) When planning the larger units of preaching, which I do on a quarterly basis, I not only review my previous sermonic efforts but also consult with staff and lay leaders about those facets of our church's life that will need emphasis during that period. Obviously I am personally counseling individuals and administering programs that deal with these same needs, thus my emerging pulpit strategy becomes integral to my total pastoral work. In other words, what I say on Sunday is decided by the same dynamics that determines what I put in the church paper on Monday, discuss in the staff meeting on Tuesday, pray about at the midweek service on Wednesday, authorize expenditures for on Thursday, or schedule a conference to consider on Friday.

(3) When the preparation of an individual sermon begins, every step in the homiletical process is guided by the criterion of intentionality. For example, the exegetical work is done in such a way as to seek from the text a reflection of its original strategy in

addressing a particular life setting with the gospel. The structural work attempts to ensure that the hearers will see clearly the target at which the sermon aims (and perceive that it is painted just over their hearts). The hortatory work evaluates each illustration much as modern scholarship has taught us to treat the parable, not as a timeless truth on some abstract topic but as a pericope which uses artful indirection to penetrate the defenses of its hearers at their most vulnerable point. All of this work is finally gathered up into a statement of objective which defines the sermon in terms of what it intends to accomplish. Until that objective has been clarified, the sermon is not ready to preach.

(4) After the sermon is delivered, its effectiveness is evaluated in light of the thrust which it has given to the ministry agenda addressed. Its physical remains are interred in a filing cabinet with tabs which, again, correspond to the outline in the appendix. This means that when reusing previously prepared sermons, I can locate and rework them in relation to everything else I have preached on a particular objective. Each year's pulpit work is recorded by this same classification system so that annually I can evaluate with our Worship Committee whether the people are receiving a balanced diet.

Let me see if I can gather up most of these strands in a recent typical illustration. During November 1982, our church observed a three-week World Mission Emphasis, for which my pulpit contribution was to be two Sunday morning sermons. Several months prior to this time our associate pastor, who has staff responsibility for the ministry system on mission service, met with the Missions Committee, the leadership of our men's and women's mission organizations, and the pastors of our three mission congregations to hammer out plans for this project. Our overall purpose, of course, was to get more of the church "on mission" in terms of the familiar triad of action projects, financial support, and prayer concern. But our specific objectives for 1982 focused on a more adequate response to poverty in the light both of mounting world hunger and of deepening local recession. All of this work was mediated to me in such forms as committee minutes, staff discussions, *Church Chimes* publicity, and supervisory conferences with the associate pastor.

When I sat down to plan the preaching input for this project, all of the preliminary work was before me. I knew everything from the theme that would appear on the posters to the decorations that would be used at the banquet. My sermonic task was to infuse all of this preparation with biblical meaning, to provide contemporary insight into the world's desperate plight, and to fortify the will to act courageously in the face of daunting obstacles. I went to the "barrel" and quickly reviewed all that I had preached on missions during my eight years in Shreveport, plus the unused sermons in this area from previous pastorates. A glance at the sermon-idea notebook reminded me of which "seed corn" might be ready for planting at this season. I perused my topical file of clippings on missions, as well as the relevant books on my study shelves. In all of this, I was looking not only for suitable sermon content which is an obvious necessity but even more for a sermon strategy, that is, for a trajectory that would "lock in" my message on that target which is the particular people to whom I preach.

I am not certain that the resulting sermons were exceptional in themselves. The titles were not very catchy, the outlines were not very ingenious, the illustrations were not very dramatic. If those sermons had any strength, it was because they were undergirded by everything that a host of dedicated people had been endeavoring to do for months. These selfless workers were my unseen pulpit allies in defining both individual and corporate needs, in proposing possible strategies for consideration, in permeating the congregational environment with a readiness to really hear what I had to say. At the same time, I was perceived by those mission leaders as their ally in summoning our church to a true sense of service. From the high visibility of the pulpit, I was seen putting my office, my personal concern, and my preaching of the Word of God behind their earnest efforts. This perception of a mutually shared ministry is very valuable not only in overcoming the loneliness of the pulpit but also in encouraging both lay and staff members who often feel that they work in isolation from the pastor's influence.

"Coordinating preaching with church objectives," to return to the title of this paper, is not merely a matter of achieving greater efficiency or of operating out of a tidy system where everything falls into place. Rather, it is a matter of learning how to make the sermon, not an end in itself but an instrument for building New Testament churches. It is a matter of learning how to integrate all of the roles of pastoral leadership into one harmonious life-style rather than segregating these roles so that they war with each other. Ultimately, it is a matter of preaching intentionally rather than impulsively, holistically rather than haphazardly, proportionately rather than preferentially. I commend such an approach to your consideration.

Appendix: An Agenda for Preaching

I. **Worship**
   As a divine creation, the church must live in the presence and power of the triune God. Worship seeks to establish, maintain, and deepen that transcendent dimension so that the people of God will live out their calling radiant in his glory, courageous in his strength, and united in his love.
   A. Public worship
      1. The gathered church as the realm of reconciliation where unity in the body of Christ manifests a solidarity beyond all human divisions
      2. The proclamation of the authoritative Word that binds its hearers together in a common confession
      3. The celebration of the coming kingdom anticipated in the Lord's Supper
   B. Personal worship
      1. The individual's need of God, hunger for God, and dependence on God
      2. The practice of private prayer and family devotions in the development of a contemplative life-style
      3. The Spirit-filled life of consecration that nourishes God-centeredness rather than self-centeredness

II. **Outreach**
   The experience of God in worship produces a compulsion to

share him with others. Since faith cannot be inherited, the church lives from one generation to the next on the effectiveness with which it brings persons to God through Jesus Christ in the convicting power of the Holy Spirit.

A. The divine initiative
1. The loving concern of God to redeem his creation by calling all persons into a saving relationship with himself
2. The urgent responsibility of the redeemed to serve as agents of God's salvation through a compassionate witness to the lost
3. The plan by which God has provided new life to all who will receive it through the finished work of Christ

B. The human response
1. Repentance from sin, commitment to Christ, and confession of faith as the way out of guilt, judgment, and condemnation
2. Baptism as the central enactment of identification with Christ in his saving death and resurrection
3. Incorporation into the body of Christ by new and unaffiliated believers as the context of continuing salvation

III. **Nurture**

Once a person has been assimilated into the household of faith, a steady process of growth toward spiritual maturity should result. This quest for Christlikeness is the goal both of each member and of the body as a whole.

A. Growth in belief
1. The place of divine inspiration and of human insight in understanding spiritual truth
2. The study and use of the Bible as the revealed Word of God
3. The central convictions of our faith: God, man, sin, salvation, church, creation, and consummation

B. Growth in behavior
1. Personal ethics: moral decision making, virtues and vices, character development
2. Parish ethics: relations between Christians within the

familial, congregational, and ecumenical households of
faith
   3. Public ethics: the Christian as a responsible citizen in
      but not of the world as regards political, economic, and
      social issues
IV. **Fellowship**
When spiritual growth is impeded by weakness, temptation,
and opposition, the Christian is not left to struggle alone. The
body of Christ functions as a supportive fellowship undergirding the embattled believer with resources to persevere.
   A. Protection
      1. The sources of strength and security in the never-ending
         battle with the forces of evil
      2. Admonishing the flock of God to overcome temptation
         by resisting compromise with sin
      3. Reclaiming the backslidden by a ministry of inreach to
         the indifferent and apathetic
   B. Encouragement
      1. The cultivation of a caring fellowship that bears one
         another's burdens in bonds of love
      2. The offer of comfort and courage in the face of loneliness
         and discouragement
      3. Coping with the common crises of life: sickness, suffer-
         ing, tragedy, death, grief
V. **Mission Service**
The church nurtures and sustains its members not as an end in
itself but in order that they might help others. In so doing,
Christians balance the "come" imperative of outreach that calls
people out of the world with the "go" imperative that calls them
to responsible care for that world.
   A. Benevolence
      1. The obligation of individual Christians to be ministers of
         reconciliation across barriers that divide humankind into
         hostile camps
      2. The servant role of the church in the world, offering

mercy to the downtrodden and protesting injustices that demean human dignity

3. The prophetic role of the church as a change agent in society liberating oppressive structures to serve the common good

B. Mission

1. The universal mission of the church in its local, regional, national, and international dimensions

2. Cooperative missions in its denominational and ecumenical expressions

3. Relationships with other religions and with civic/charitable service agencies in fulfilling the mission of the church

VI. Administration

Spirit requires structure to channel and conserve its enduring impact. Therefore, the church must be not only a living organism but an institutional organization giving visible form to its ministries in the world of time and space.

A. Human resources

1. The nature of the church as a priesthood of believers utilizing and distributing the spiritual gifts of all its members for mutual edification

2. The organization of the church to facilitate the accomplishment of its tasks

3. The leadership of the church in such roles as ministers and deacons

B. Material resources

1. The place of tangible realities as aids to an intangible faith

2. The financial stewardship of systematic giving through tithes and special offerings

3. The erection and care of facilities as a focal place to facilitate the ministries of the church

Your Place in Your Church
Acts 2:46

It is my custom to use these annual anniversary occasions to bring a message on "The State of the Church." Rather than reviewing the successes and failures of the past year, I attempt instead to define the cutting edge of our corporate life, to assess any changes needed in our current priorities, and to suggest the goals toward which we should press during the months ahead.

My comments this year are based directly on two messages delivered at this time last year: first, my third anniversary sermon on "The Purpose of the Church," preached on September 10, 1978;[1] second, a sermon on "The Cruciality of the Sunday School," preached on October 1, 1978, in connection with the call of John Sisemore to lead our program staff.[2] After almost a year of testing these two foundational approaches, I am now ready to update and enlarge my perspective by combining them into a unified understanding of what I deeply believe should be our primary task during the next twelve months.

I. A Purpose with a Plan

Since you could hardly be expected to recall the details of two sermons preached nearly twelve months ago, let me summarize the main points of each in such a way as to show why I now wish to link them together.

In "The Purpose of the Church," I sought to be specific about the "marks" of a true body of believers, identifying those essential components without which we can never lay claim to the central Baptist axiom of being a "New Testament Church." I devoted a great deal of thought to this definition because purposes determine long-range goals which, in turn, shape short-range objectives. They also test the adequacy of our entire endeavor by providing a checklist which measures whether our programs of ministry are both comprehensive and balanced. After an additional year of searching the Scriptures, reviewing church history, pondering Christian doctrine, and evaluating the full range of our practical activities, I am more convinced than ever that any church committed to declare "The Whole Word to the Whole World" must be engaged in the following:[3]

(1) Worship: the cultivation of a transcendent encounter with God so that divine power will energize both the church in fulfilling its mission on earth and each believer in living a Spirit-filled life of consecration;

(2) Outreach: the discovery of personal salvation in Jesus Christ and the sharing of that salvation both with the lost and with the unaffiliated living within reach of our influence;

(3) Nurture: the development both of the body and of its members to attain "the measure of the stature of the fulness of Christ" (Eph. 4:13), so that the spiritually mature may exercise their gifts in guiding the spiritually immature to grow in grace.

(4) Pastoral Care: the cultivation of a caring fellowship sustained by bonds of love so that each individual will feel the undergirding and encouragement of fellow Christians in coping victoriously with the struggles of life;

(5) Service: the church acting collectively as a public institution and individually as a private citizenry to challenge the corrupt structures of society, to liberate the oppressed, and to extend the righteousness of God around the world through missionary and benevolent work;

(6) Administration: the mobilization of the church's human and material resources to facilitate its mission to each member, to the congregation as a whole, and to the world which it serves.

Notice that in each of these six definitions of purpose a necessary balance has been struck between the church viewed collectively as one body and the church viewed individually as many members (see 1 Cor. 12:27). Christianity is an intensely personal faith which is experienced at the depth of one's being, but it is also a profoundly corporate reality in which all of those committed to Christ discover their inescapable solidarity with each other in bonds of love. The Christian life is like an ellipse with two focuses, one inward and the other outward, one singular and the other social, one existential and the other relational. This means that what happens to the church as a whole and to each of its parts are equally important. Therefore, we must structure our organized expression of the Christian faith to give balanced attention to each of these focuses, thereby insuring that our six purposes will be fulfilled both for the entire fellowship as an organic unity and for each of its participants as an individual person.

It was to this imperative that I addressed my second sermon on "The Cruciality of the Sunday School." That sequel advanced three reasons why our church must not only be organized into one large congregation but must also be organized into many small groups: (1) biblically, only this pattern corresponds to the centrality of one large unifying Temple in the Old Testament balanced by the centrality of many small "house churches" in the New Testament (see Acts 2:46); (2) theologically, it is only in small clusters that we are able to cultivate a manageable number of relationships through which to fulfill the priesthood of every believer; (3) practically, only the variety possible in many small units permits a healthy diversification based on such inherent human differences as age, sex, and domestic circumstances.

Lying behind all three of the emphases in that sermon was the realization that three thousand people simply cannot function as a New Testament church when organized only as one large congregation. To be sure, there are those willing to flock by the thousands to some charismatic minister, such as an "electronic church" celebrity.[4]

Many will go as far as to join a superchurch spawned by media stardom and to devote exclusive loyalty to a pastor who rules his empire as a spiritual autocrat. But there are very few ministers able to build a large church exclusively around themselves, and fewer still willing to do so even if they could. The New Testament has its spiritual giants, such as the apostle Paul, but it knows nothing of a mass movement of hero worshipers following some prominent religious personality as part of a crowd. When the multitudes tried to do that to Jesus, he turned his back on them and organized instead a band of twelve (Mark 3:7-19)!

All of this does not mean that there should be no large churches, but it does mean that a large church is legitimate only when it has many small cells within it. How small, you ask? Small enough for every prospect to be noticed the first time that he or she attends. Small enough for every member to be missed as soon as he or she becomes inactive. Small enough for the group to keep up with the little hurts as well as the major crises that come to every life. Small enough to plan a mission action project that will succeed only if every person participates. Small enough to know each person's name and something about his or her family situation. Small enough to meet in each other's homes and not just in large church buildings. How may we create many small churches within our one large church?

II. Toward a New Definition of Sunday School

To answer that question, we must hammer out a new understanding of Sunday School which differs significantly from our traditional conception. In the past, Baptists have customarily thought of the Sunday School as one organization among many within the church, the educational arm devoted to lay study of the Bible. After all, the basic unit was called a "class," the leader was called a "teacher," and the agenda was called a "lesson." All of this implied that the basic purpose was to explain passages of Scripture and then apply their truths to daily living. On this model, the key qualification of leaders was an ability to impart Bible knowledge, and the key responsibility of members was a willingness to be good "pupils." In short, as the historic name implied, "Sunday School" meant simply going to a Bible school on Sunday.

I feel no particular need to change this deeply entrenched terminology, but I do want to challenge the stereotype which it supports. For what I am proposing is that we view Sunday School not as a school on Sunday but as manageably small units of the church organized for ministry on every day of the week. This enlarged definition would mean that a "teacher" is not simply a teacher but is an enabler or equipper of the members in their quest for spiritual fulfillment. It would mean that a "lesson" is not simply a lesson but is a continuing search for biblical guidance in accomplishing every purpose for which the church exists. It would mean that a "pupil" is not simply a pupil but is a disciple (or would-be disciple) learning to express Christian commitment in the context of responsible relationships.

This understanding would set the Sunday School apart as different not only in degree but also in kind from every other organization of the church. It is not that Sunday School classes are more important than choirs or mission circles or recreational teams. Rather, I am suggesting that we view the Sunday School as something unique, namely, the way in which one large church is organized into many small churches. On this approach, every other organization and activity exists to support and enrich the church both in its large-group and in its small-group expression. To adapt a classic theological distinction, I would so define the Sunday School that it belongs to the "being" (esse) of the church whereas other organizations within the congregation belong to the "well-being" (bene esse) of the church.

Let me try to explain as simply as possible why I have been driven to this deeper understanding of the Sunday School. My contention has nothing to do with the expediencies of ministerial salesmanship; that is, I am not advancing a new idea in order to promote increased Sunday School participation. Rather, I am trying to base my thinking on what the New Testament churches were actually like, and I know from my Bible that they were small bands of believers who shared life together at its deepest level. But in coming to the First Baptist Church in Shreveport I inherited a quite different reality, a vastly larger body in which many members had no contact at all with each other. When I asked, "How can I help this congregation to function as a New Testament church?" only two answers emerged: either break up its one large membership into dozens of small, independent fellowships or find some way to organize its entire membership into many separate but interlocking modules, each one of them small enough to become an authentic expression of New Testament Christianity within our collective life.

There are several reasons why I opted for the latter course of action. Obviously it would be traumatic to scatter our large flock and begin meeting away from this centralized campus as a series of "house churches." My own professional career would be jeopardized by such drastic decentralization since obviously a handful of believers could not possibly support even one pastor and his family, much less our large staff of specialists. We would all have to become itinerant ministers, I suppose, living off the gifts of many groups as did Paul and his companions in New Testament times. But the overriding reason for my strategy is not the personal security to be found in a large church. Rather, it is grounded in the insight that the Bible contains two basic models for organizing the people of God, the Old Testament model of one large Temple and the New Testament model of many small fellowships. And at the theological midpoint where these two models met, on the boundary between Judaism and Christianity, they coexisted together within the life of the earliest church (Acts 2:46)![5]

What this means, quite candidly, is that I want us to have the best of both worlds, the strength of a stable temple and the warmth of friendly home, the cohesiveness of a united institution and the diversity of a hundred different cell groups, the social impact of a large membership and the personal intimacy of a small membership. This is a way of saying that if we had no plan for organizing our large church into small units I would insist that we invent one. But since we already have the Sunday School as the one organization which provides a small-group experience of Christian discipleship for every member and prospect, I suggest that we utilize it to help us become a functioning New Testament church, which is our central purpose. The framework is already here if only we will liberate its restricted image and infuse it with a new sense of destiny equal to its highest potential.

American Christianity in the last half of the twentieth century has been deeply polarized by two conflicting approaches to basic strategy. On the one hand, there are those who would seize on the media revolution to create superchurches of vast sizes seldom known before.[6] On the other hand, there are those who would counter this trend by pleading for "renewal" in terms of relational integrity, fashioning remnant bands in which confessional dialogue replaces the imperial pulpit and disciplined love is more important than statistical success.[7] While the extremes of these two positions can hardly be harmonized, there is no need to make a rigid choice between their two basic emphases.[8] With the right kind of Sunday School, we can become as large a church as the response of our community permits and yet offer every member a unit within our church small enough to experience the full range of New Testament religion.

To illustrate the seriousness with which I view this model, let me here anticipate a pastoral recommendation which I am developing for congregational consideration. In the past, when people "joined the church," we put their name only on a general membership roll. But if life in our church must be both a large- and a small-group experience, why not automatically enroll them in Sunday School as well? If we really believe that every person needs balanced participation both in "big church" and in "little church," we can adopt the policy that membership in the First Baptist Church, Shreveport, involves affiliation with both expressions of our congregational life. To be sure, some want to join only the church and not the Sunday School, while others want to join only the Sunday School and not the church. But it is the responsibility of our congregation to decide on a definition of church membership true to our deepest nature and purpose, and I am convinced that it should involve the dual alignment just described.[9] I fully realize that this would load our Sunday School rolls with a host of inactive and even nonresident members, but why not let each of our basic ministry units share with the entire body a small part of the burden of reaching the backslidden for active service? Indeed, what could be a more effective strategy than to break down one huge problem into manageable segments that no longer intimidate or overwhelm?

III. A Balanced Vision of the Ministering Church

We are now in a position to understand the creative step which I am urging us to take by synthesizing the insights of the two sermons summarized at the outset of this message. In terms of formal logic, my proposal may be stated as a simple syllogism. The major premise is that every true church must fulfill at least six essential functions. The minor premise is that every large church must also have many small cells within it. The inescapable conclusion, therefore, is that these six purposes must be fulfilled for the entire body through the church in its centralized expression but for each individual member through the church in its decentralized expression. That being so, your place in your church may be defined as balanced participation both in the body as a whole and in the appropriate cell group which it provides for persons of every age, sex, and circumstance.

Let me conclude with a very sketchy vision of how I see our six essential purposes being fulfilled at these two levels of congregational life. I do this in order to reinforce my conclusion that you need equal involvement in each of these dimensions in order to have a whole-orbed Christian experience.

(1) Worship: the gathering of the many should express the unity of our corporate body in obedience to one Word and in communion with one Lord, whereas the gathering of the few should provide a relaxed, informal setting in which to learn how to practice the presence of God through personal prayer and meditation.

(2) Outreach: the larger church should proclaim the gospel through intensive efforts that attract the attention of the entire community and awaken the concern of the lost, whereas the smaller church should offer each prospect a home for faith where he or she is loved as a sinner saved by grace.

(3) Nurture: the heterogeneous whole should fulfill the ministry of reconciliation by which we all learn to recognize and rejoice in our great diversity, whereas each of the more homogeneous parts should minister to the developmental needs of its particular age and sex.

(4) Pastoral Care: the total flock should rally in support of those passing through the great crises of life such as birth, marriage,

illness, and death, whereas the more intimate flock should provide a sustaining network of concern in dealing with the daily cares of life.

(5) Service: the entire army of the Lord should march against entrenched evil in the united strength of a worldwide missionary organization, whereas the soldiers in each platoon of that army should be taught "hand-to-hand combat" in attacking the enemies of the gospel with which they come in contact.

(6) Administration: the centralized organization of the church should provide such support services for ministry as facilities, budget, and staff, whereas the decentralized organization should focus on the stewardship responsibility of each individual in contributing a proportionate share of both human and material resources to the entire enterprise.

Two imperatives lie immediately before us, each of them with two aspects. First, we must guide our entire congregation to fulfill its mission as the unified expression of a New Testament church, while at the same time guiding each unit of our Sunday School to fulfill its mission as the small-group expression of a New Testament church. Second, we must challenge each individual to become a true member both of our larger body and of the appropriate constituent cell. When each of us defines our place in that fashion, we will begin to discover true spiritual fulfillment and our church will begin to achieve its highest purposes under God.

Notes

1. William E. Hull, "The Purpose of the Church," First Baptist Church, 10 Sep. 1978, Shreveport Sermon #138.

2. William E. Hull, "The Cruciality of the Sunday School," First Baptist Church, 1 Oct. 1978, Shreveport Sermon #141.

3. For a brief summary and interpretation see William E. Hull, "The Purpose of Our Church," *Church Chimes*, First Baptist Church, 16 Sep. 1978, vol. 61, no. 38, p. 3.

4. On this burgeoning new movement see William E. Hull, "The Electronic Church," *Church Chimes*, First Baptist Church, 24 Mar. 1979, vol. 62, no. 12, p. 3.

5. The point of the argument here is not that the most primitive expression of early Christianity is necessarily the best. Rather, it is that, under certain circumstances, the "Temple" model and the "house church" model for organizing the people of God may legitimately overlap. Such circumstances were present in Acts 2:46, they have been present repeatedly in Christian history, and I find them present in The First Baptist Church of Shreveport at this point in my ministry. Although the model of one large temple-type church with many small house-type churches within it is particularly suited to balance the prevailing ecclesiological pattern in the Old Testament with that in the New Testament, I would not conclude from this that such a model should be normative for all church life today. Rather, I see the rich diversity of church polity throughout the Bible offering us a wide variety of options with which to experiment, any of them legitimate that expresses the true intentionality of Scripture for our particular circumstances. On the fallacies of "primitivism" in theories of repristination see Robert L. Wilken, *The Myth of Christian Beginnings* (Garden City: Doubleday, 1971). On the need for flexibility in applying biblical guidelines to contemporary organization see W. D. Davies, "A Normative Pattern of Church Life In the New Testament?" *Christian Origins and Judaism* (Philadelphia: Westminster, 1962), pp. 199-229.

6. The "superchurch" movement has been described by Elmer Towns, *The Ten Largest Sunday Schools and What Makes Them Grow* (Grand Rapids: Baker, 1969); *America's Fastest Growing Churches* (Nashville: Impact Books, 1972). On the media aspect of the movement see Ben Armstrong, *The Electric Church* (Nashville: Thomas Nelson, 1979). A more moderate expression of this tendency is the "Church Growth Movement" centered in the American Institute for Church Growth, Pasadena, California, whose approach is reflected in the writings of Donald McGavran, Peter Wagner, and Win Arn.

7. The "Church Renewal Movement" was popularized by the writings of Elton Trueblood, such as *The Company of the Committed* (New York: Harper & Brothers, 1961). The more extreme manifestation of the movement may be seen in the Church of the Saviour, Washington, DC, led by Gordon Cosby and described in the writings of Elizabeth O'Connor, such as *Call to Commitment* (New York: Harper & Row, 1963). The more moderate expression of the "Church Renewal Movement," comparable to the place of the American Institute for Church Growth in the "Church Growth Movement," is the approach of Faith at Work, reflected in the writings of Lyman Coleman, Bruce Larson, Keith Miller, and Ralph Osborne. The earlier emphases of Elton Trueblood are perpetuated by the Yokefellow Associates organization in Richmond, Indiana.

8. To some extent I am suggesting that the "en-*large*-ment" concerns rooted in the centrifugal thrust of the "Church Growth Movement" may be expressed through the dynamics of large church life while the "en-*small*-ment" concerns rooted in the centripetal thrust of the "Church Renewal Movement" may be expressed through the dynamics of small church life (i.e. Sunday School). This hint of accommodation is in sharp contrast to the adversary relationship which these emphases have typically sustained to each other. For a biblical and theological rationale in support of rapprochement see William E. Hull, "The Renewal of the Church" (Shreveport: First Baptist Church, October 19, 1975), Shreveport Sermon #9.

9. Polity should, of course, rest on sound doctrine, and I regret that there is not

space here to sketch the ecclesiology of my contention. We are accustomed to distinguish between one "universal church" and many "local churches," while recognizing an essential unity between them. My suggestion here is that the spiritual reality which makes that "one-in-many" relationship possible also permits us to think of one local church as having many diverse manifestations of ecclesial reality in a host of Sunday School classes. In other words, the ecumenical issue concerns not only the relation of a local church to the many churches *beyond* it but also the relation of that local church to the many churches *within* it. The theological underpinnings of this approach have been well described by P. T. Forsyth, *The Church and the Sacraments* (London: Independent Press, 1917), pp. 65-70. Forsyth argues that, ultimately, there is only one churchly reality, which is defined by the presence of Christ among his people. This reality may be universal in the sense that Christ dwells with all Christians everywhere to the end of the age. It may be local in that this total and continuous church may "outcrop" in a particular place, "the Whole Church, as it were, [rushing] to the spot touched by the presence of Christ" (p. 66). But it may also be where two or three are gathered in Christ's name (Matt. 18:20), and he comes to bring all Christendon (p. 66). Forsyth concludes: "and the church in a private house (i.e. in a small group expression) was as much *the* church as the whole Christianity of Corinth" (p. 70).

8

Narrative Preaching

Alton H. McEachern

Winston Jones wrote, "Story-telling is the most ancient of the arts, and the most universal."[1]

Preaching is a demanding task. George Buttrick said, "The Lord Christ has his preachers at hard labor." William Barclay insisted that preachers should be chained to their desks four morning a week and forbidden to rise until they have produced something worthwhile to show for their labors. He also said that if we cannot put fire into our sermons, we should put our sermons in the fire. No person can approach preaching without some degree of anxiety.

We share a high view of the importance of preaching. Indeed, there is strong biblical argument for the sacramental nature of the preaching event (1 Cor. 1:21-23; Rom. 10:14-15,17). D. M. Baillie contends that "we stand between a memory and a hope, looking backward to the incarnation and forward to the consummation."[2] Inspired preaching makes both events contemporary.

While preaching is demanding, its joys are also great. I am "terribly glad" to be a preaching pastor. Buttrick argued that "only the pastor, or a man with pastoral imagination can preach."[3] In his Lyman Beecher lectures David H. C. Read contended that "the preacher is a Moses who never gets the children of Israel off his back and doesn't want to. He's not the impresario who says to his secretary, 'Tell that nuisance to go to hell—I'm composing a masterpiece on Christian love.' . . . He is sent from God to live with people, talk with them, listen to them, feel what they feel, and only after he has been through the dusty streets does he mount the pulpit steps. Like his Lord he must be responsive to that tug on the sleeve when he is at his busiest." Read says that the entire Bible

151

stands witness to the pastor-preacher as the "man sent from God."[4]

Dogma Is Drama

Dorothy Sayers made high drama of biblical material. After writing twelve passion plays, she said, "The Christan faith is the most exciting drama that has ever staggered the imagination of man—and the dogma is the drama." She found the gospel narratives anything but dull: "Any journalist hearing it for the first time would recognize it as news; those who did hear it for the first time did call it . . . good news."[5] Why then is so much modern preaching anything but interesting and exciting? One reason is that it has lost its dramatic narrative character. The drama we find in the Bible is interesting, universal, and timeless.

One of the great needs of biblical preaching is the need to be contemporary. Narrative preaching is a variant which elaborates the basic biblical materials and creates a sense of contemporaneity. Both the personality and the life situation of the biblical character come alive for the hearer. The dramatic monologue sermon allows the biblical personality to speak in the first person. Listeners may well feel that they are reliving the biblical event. Thus, the Word comes alive in the experience of the hearer to challenge, heal, and redeem. The hearer feels that he is there, a contemporary of biblical personality and events.

Many times worshipers are not moved by powerful biblical truths because of the truths' familiarity. The listeners have heard the narrative or parable many times since childhood. Some even think of the biblical accounts as fairy tales. This problem calls on the preacher to present his material through new and fresh methods. Narrative preaching is one approach worthy of our consideration.

The theology of the Bible is clothed in the flesh and blood of living characters. Human nature is essentially the same today as it was in biblical times. Some of the characters of the Old and New Testament walk our streets in modern dress, their temperaments and their basic problems the same as our own. Persons like Judas are sticky-fingered treasurers and bankers of our time who enrich themselves at the price of betrayal of trust. Cain still stalks modern parks and alleys. Delilah plies her trade in Paris frock or hot pants. Prejudice did not die with Simon Peter at Caesarea. Salome dances atop French quarter bars, and Potiphar is preppy. Canaanite fertility cults are practiced by pill-liberated suburban housewives. Modern preaching dare not do less than clothe theological truth in flesh and blood.

Christian worship at its best is dramatic and exciting, though not necessarily theatrical. The church has largely lost its sense of the dramatic nature of the gospel. The ordinances of baptism and Lord's Supper are powerful symbolic presentations of gospel truth. They appeal to all the human senses and have a dramatic quality.

Narrative preaching tends to heighten interest in the message and thus enhance communication. While it should not become the only form of preaching, it can add variety and spice to the congregation's sermonic diet.

Narrative preaching is in the finest biblical tradition. Henry Grady Davis contends that the gospel itself is made up principally of narration. It is a series of accounts of people, places, and happenings, not simply rational arguments. Modern preaching appears to have reversed the percentages: while the gospel is nine tenths narration, most of our sermons are nine tenths exhortation.

Many biblical ideas were first presented in story form. It is easier to remember a story than an ordinary sermon or even a poem. The prophets and other Old Testament writers were master storytellers, as was Jesus. His parables are vivid stories that stick in the mind.

A well-told story still has great appeal. Children beg their parents to read or tell them a story. Adults almost universally enjoy "a good story." Theater and the television industry are built on human interest in stories. A good story can capture the essence of an event and hold it before the hearers for either entertainment or instruction.

The preacher will be wise to capitalize on the dramatic nature of the gospel and our natural interest in drama. Jesus made people see the truth by simple stories. The modern preacher's task is much the same. Skillfully done, narrative preaching, including the dramatic monologue, can improve the effective communication of the gospel. It gets and holds the congregation's attention. It creates a high level of interest in the message. Narrative preaching can be an effective teaching device, conveying Bible knowledge, as well as stirring the emotions and moving the will of the hearers.

Considerations in Narrative Preaching

The use of imagination has an important place in narrative preaching. This type of sermon calls for filling in the gaps not covered in the biblical narrative. The preacher has more opportunity to make use of his imagination in dramatic preaching than in other types. He is at liberty to create the feelings and emotions of the character, as well as to describe the setting. He will be careful that his imagination does not violate the biblical account.

The narrative sermon can create suspense. People will listen eagerly. Spurgeon called the use of imagination in preaching "surprise power."

I have found that the fruits of critical Bible study can often be introduced into a sermon by imagining the life situation of a biblical character.

One problem in narrative preaching is the danger of anachronism. By this I mean putting things into the character's life and speech that could not have been true to his time. It is very easy to let untimely references or jargon slip into the narration. This is always a literary problem. The King James Version of the Bible speaks of candlesticks instead of lampstands. Shakespeare had a clock stroke in his play Julius Caesar, though clocks had not yet been invented. One must be sure to check the historical accuracy of the facts included in narrative preaching.

This type preaching also requires careful research and preparation on the part of the preacher. You will want to be as familiar as possible with the times in which the character lived, striving for historical accuracy. The objective of confronting persons with the claims of the gospel requires the preacher's very best effort in both preparation and delivery.

How-to

You will want to make careful research notes, giving attention to your sources. After the basic research is complete, give it some time to mellow. The entire sermon idea may be put on a back burner until a central theme surfaces. Frederick Speakman says that it often requires a month for him to write a dramatic monologue sermon.

Once you've found the key for the sermon, organize your facts and narrative around it. Do not be afraid to eliminate good material in favor of the best. Ideally, a sermon should run not more than twenty to twenty-five minutes. You can't have a character relate all the facts you know about him in that brief span. Therefore, you will choose only the most important facts which fit your theme. Severe pruning can make the sermon more effective. No one will be impressed by being told all the preacher knows at a single sitting. Remember to deal with only the central aspect of the character.

You may choose to write out your manuscript or use what Clyde Fant calls the "oral manuscript" in preparation for delivery. Writing will help to polish phrases and maintain a conversational style. Use short sentences and simple, strong words. Write the introduction and conclusion carefully and commit them to memory.

The introduction sets the scene and introduces the speaking character, as well as those to whom he is speaking. This helps prepare the congregation for what is to follow.

Write out the narrative in simple language. You will want to use active colorful verbs and vivid descriptions of people and places. Always be faithful to the biblical material.

I find that the sermon needs to be rehearsed both mentally and verbally in order to have it clearly in mind. There is hardly any way to speak effectively in the first person or to deliver an exciting narrative while reading from extensive notes or a manuscript. It is not necessary to memorize the sermon word for word, though a few persons have such a gift. Only the key passages need to be memorized—the pegs on which the narrative hangs. A key word or phrase can act as a transitional device and trigger the preacher's memory to recall the next section of the sermon. W. E. Sangster contended that the preacher should learn to "think paragraphically."

In delivery the narrative sermon may be addressed to an imaginary person. Dramatic techniques of flashback and reverie may be employed as well. Conversational tone is usually best for use in this type preaching. However, conversational speech need not lack excitement and emotion.

You may want to create the scene verbally or on occasion make proper use of lighting, costume, and makeup. It appears that the use of costume is more effective in the evening service than in the morning. Children, youth, and young adults have a greater appreciation for the use of costume than do middle or older adults.

One of the weaknesses in dramatic preaching is at the point of the application of biblical truth. The application has to be self-evident or implicit rather than explicit. It is awkward for the preacher to step out of character and apply the sermon's spiritual truths to modern life situations. Most hearers are more capable of making their own application than we preachers think.

One way to begin narrative preaching is not to attempt an entire sermon. Start with a vivid introduction to a more conventional sermon. You may try painting a word picture of a biblical scene, such as Peter's call beside the Sea of Galilee or the siege of Jerusalem or the wailing of the songless Israelite captives in Babylon. After you feel comfortable with the method, it can be expanded and used for a full-length sermon.

The Advent and Easter seasons lend themselves naturally to dramatic preaching. It can be great fun and may provide a fresh and effective tool for communicating the gospel.

The late J. Wallace Hamilton of Florida gave us some words which can be aptly applied to narrative preaching. He wrote: "Clarity, poetry, vitality! We must make it clear; we must make it sing; and above it all we must make it live."[6]

Notes

1. Winston Jones, *Preaching and the Dramatic Arts* (New York: The Macmillan Co., 1948), p. 106.

2. D. M. Baillie, *Theology of the Sacraments* (New York: Charles Scribner's Sons, 1957), p. 102.

3. George Buttrick, *Sermons Preached in a University Church* (Nashville: Abingdon, 1957), p. 7.

4. David H. C. Read, *Sent From God* (Nashville: Abingdon, 1974), pp. 69-70.

5. Dorothy Sayers, *The Greatest Drama Ever Staged* (London: Hodder and Stoughton, 1938), pp. 17, 24.

6. J. Wallace Hamilton, *Still the Trumpet Sounds* (Old Tappan: Fleming H. Revell, 1970), p. 159.

The Distant Disciple—Nicodemus
John 3:12-16; 7:45-53; 19:38-42

"Shalom! Let me introduce myself. I am a member of an old family in Jerusalem. We can trace our lineage back to the time when our nation returned from the Exile in Babylon. My family was prominent, especially during the time of Maccabean rule.

"As a guardian of the establishment, I belong to an elite religious sect within Judaism. We call ourselves Pharisees, or the 'separated ones.' We are a strict brotherhood made up of the best of our people and pledged to obey the law and uphold the traditions of our fathers. We consider ourselves to be the true Israelites. We believe in the resurrection of the dead and look forward to the coming of the Messiah. My brothers expect him to be a militant figure who will drive the Romans from our holy city.

"Because of my position in the community, I am also on the seventy-member Jewish supreme court, the Sanhedrin. The Roman governor allows us considerable jurisdiction over the internal government of the province. Our religious authority extends to every Jewish male in the world. The high priest himself is our president or chief justice. My membership in this body marks me as a ruler of the Jews.

"I have quite a reputation as a rabbi or teacher among my people. Some give me the title, 'The Teacher.' My chief teacher was Gamaliel, of whom you may have heard!

"Modesty has never been exactly a virtue among my brotherhood. Therefore, allow me to say that I represent the quintessence of Judaism, or the Jewish faith.

"I have always considered myself a practical, rational man. I pride myself on being not only a good and obedient son of Abraham but

158

also a fair one. Above everything else, a ruler must be fair!

At Passover some five springs ago, we had quite a stir in the capital. An intense young rabbi from Galilee came to the feast accompanied by a group of his students or disciples. He caused quite a ruckus by driving the sellers of sacrificial animals and birds out of the Temple complex—with a plaited whip! He also upset the tables of the money changers. It very nearly precipitated a riot. The high priest was livid! He had licensed the stalls and received a handsome commission on their profits.

"However, what really upset my party, the Pharisees, was what this fellow Jesus said as he cleared the place out. 'You shall not make my Father's house a house of trade!'

"His Father's house, indeed. Who did he think he was? That was what my fellow Pharisees wanted to know. Then it was reported that he said he would destroy the Temple and rebuild it in three days. An absurd claim, we thought.

"My group was up in arms against this fellow Jesus. 'But let us be fair,' I said. 'Let's examine all the facts.' Jesus did a number of miracles, or 'signs,' as he called them. I didn't put much stock in them, until my blind cousin was healed by him. It was an authentic miracle. From that moment I knew we must take this rabbi seriously. Our writings say that if a prophet gives a sign or a miracle he is to be listened to.

"Let me confess that despite my family's wealth and my own prominence as a rabbi in Jerusalem something was lacking to me. I have kept the law all my adult life. Yet there was little joy in it all. It was largely an external affair of ritual cleanliness and righteousness. At a deeper level I had been a seeker after truth for some time before I met the Master. I certainly had a veneer of respectability, but underneath I felt a nagging void. I determined to meet Jesus and examine his claims and teachings for myself. After all, it was the only fair thing to do.

"I decided to arrange an interview with Jesus. I had to go by night. There were several reasons for this. Night was the favorite time for rabbis to discuss the law and theology among themselves. It was a quiet time when there would be little likelihood of interruption. Further, the visit must be kept confidential. He was a highly controversial person. Discretion dictated that the interview be conducted privately.

"As I have thought about that interview since that night, I realize that I came to Jesus out of spiritual darkness as well.

"I shall never forget that warm spring evening. I had made arrangements with one of his disciples, Andrew, for the interview. He met me at the door of the guest house and said his master was waiting for me on the flat roof. I climbed the outside stair with pounding heart. Why should a man of my position be so excited about meeting this humble Galilean? Maybe it was some deep longing inside me or perhaps some sort of premonition that tonight could be of eternal importance.

"I arrived at the roof to see him standing in the moonlight. He came forward to receive me. I expected him to be tired and bedraggled. Andrew had astutely indicated that he had been teaching and healing since daybreak. However, Jesus looked completely rested and composed; much more than I, after climbing the steps. Stairs were never my favorite invention. He looked so young! He couldn't have been more than thirty. His eyes were piercing, even by moonlight. His sharp intelligence fairly flashed from those clear eyes. He looked like a king!

"Once I'd caught my breath and regained my composure I began the conversation politely.

"'Rabbi,' I said, 'we know that you are a teacher come from God; for no one can do these signs that you do, unless God is with him.' I approached him as one theologian to another, speaking for the Jewish religious establishment.

"His reply shocked me. He said, 'Amen, amen, I say to you, unless you are born again you cannot see the kingdom of God.' It was as though he were saying, 'Let's not talk about me and my miracles, but about you and your entry into the kingdom.' I had been diplomatic and complimentary. Jesus' reply ignored these tributes and went like a rapier to the heart of my own spiritual problem.

"I wasn't to be dealt with so abruptly. I took him quite literally and said, 'Born again? How can a man be born when he is old? Can he enter a second time into his mother's womb and be born?' My mind was whirling at the thought. The very idea! Proselytes to Judaism were said to be born again. But what need had a Hebrew to be born more than as a son of Abraham? Incredible! Once a man is old his habits and life patterns are fixed. He doesn't make such a radical change!

"Then Jesus said, 'Unless one is born of water and the Spirit, he cannot enter the kingdom of God.'

"'Born of water' conjured up vivid memories of John the Baptist and his water baptism of good Jews! What an explosion that had set off among my Pharisee brethren!

"'Born of the Spirit.' Such a thing could take place only once the Messiah had come! What could he mean?

"Then Jesus pointed out the sovereignty of the warm night wind. 'The wind blows where it wills,' he said. Now do you suppose the divine will is all that spontaneous? We thought we had God shut up in the law and our cult, our worship. Could he be bringing new truth into our stuffy Temple on the fresh ideas of this young rabbi? I couldn't be precisely sure of his meaning. He used a play on words. You see, in our language the same word means breath, wind, or spirit. It took some thinking to unravel that one.

"'How can this be?' I asked.

"Jesus wanted to make it clear that he was not talking about human birth but about spiritual birth. He seemed disappointed that I was so slow to catch his meaning. 'Nicodemus,' he said, 'are you a teacher of Israel, and yet you do not understand this?'

"Then he said—and I can never forget the words—'For God so loved the world that he gave his only Son, that whoever believes in him should not perish but have eternal life.' I did not understand the full import of those words until later—much later!

"The antithesis of faith is not doubt, but unbelief. How hard it was for me to believe that this intense young Galilean could be the Son of God—the Messiah. The interview concluded with my being in a spiritual quandary. A battle was raging inside me. I wanted to believe, yet I had so much religious tradition to 'unlearn,' as it were. I wanted to uphold what I had always known, and I wanted to

believe this radical new birth was possible for me as well. I had no
peace of mind. I wanted to declare for him, but I had too much to
give up. A prudent man is seldom at peace! That interview created a
moral dilemma for me.

"It was not until the next year at the Feast of Tabernacles in
Jerusalem that I saw Jesus again. The Sanhedrin decided to send
certain persons to investigate him. They reported to the Sanhedrin,
'No man ever spoke like this man!'

"The vast majority of the court was too blinded by prejudice
against Jesus to be fair. They asked, 'Have any of the Pharisees
believed in him? This rabble crowd, these people of the land are
accursed!'

"My heart was in my throat. I wanted to say, 'Yes, this Pharisee
believes in him!' But I didn't dare. That was not the time or the
place. The fever of their opposition to Jesus was at too high a pitch.

"Mustering all my courage, I asked, 'Does our law judge a man
without first giving him a hearing? Let's be fair!'

"But they turned on me almost to a man. 'Are you from Galilee
too?' one member screamed. 'Search the Scriptures and you will see
that no prophet comes from Galilee.' Only later did I learn that Jesus
was born in Bethlehem of Judea! They didn't think any Galilean was
ever to be taken seriously. Their contempt was something to behold.
Prejudice is never uglier than when it is religious prejudice.

"I stood alone. Never before in all my life had I felt so alone. Little
did I notice or suspect that my lame defense of Jesus had a telling
effect on one of our Sanhedrin members. Joseph, from the northern
Judean village of Arimathea, took in all I'd said. He was a good man
who was looking for the kingdom of God. He was a new member of
the council, in contrast to my old family. My defense of Jesus was
enough to set Joseph thinking.

"The next Passover was a sheer nightmare. Jesus returned to
Jerusalem in triumph to the praise of the common people. This only
served to crystallize the religious authorities' opposition to him.
They were determined to see him dead.

"An illegal meeting of the council was called in the early hours of

Friday morning. 'Conveniently' the messenger did not get word to me. I suppose they thought I might stall for time. When I heard about the trial at midmorning, I was surprised to learn one white stone had been cast. There was one other member who believed Jesus was innocent! Nevertheless, Jesus was condemned to death.

"Shortly before noon, I went outside the city wall to the place of execution. It was incredible that such a magnificent life could be snuffed out. As I watched him hanging there, suddenly I recalled something he had said to me that night. 'As Moses lifted up the serpent in the wilderness, so must the Son of man be lifted up, that whoever believes in him may have eternal life.'

"Suddenly I understood! I knew! It was true! Jesus is the Son of God! But how could it end like this—with a criminal's cross? I turned to flee. As I ran down the hill I bumped into a hooded figure. Through tears, I made out the familiar face. It was Joseph of Arimathea! He was the one who had cast the white stone—the innocent vote.

"Joseph took me over to the west side of the hill. We went up a narrow walled street and through a gate. It opened onto a quiet, lovely garden. There Joseph showed me his newly hewn family tomb. Looking eastward, I could still see the silhouette of the three crosses.

"We made our plans quietly. Joseph would procure Jesus' body from Pilate. I would meet him at the garden tomb with linen and spices for the Master's burial. We went our separate ways.

"When I returned, carrying nearly a hundred pounds of myrrh and aloes, I found Joseph there with his precious burden.

"Lovingly, we bathed the body, cleaning the wounds and the pierced brow. We laid his body on the white linen sheet and covered it. Then, pouring on the spices, we wrapped the body in winding cloths. It was a burial befitting a king—the King of the Jews. We had to work hurriedly, for the sabbath was at hand. What a scene we must have made—two secret disciples who came over to the Master's side only after his death! It is a sad, almost tragic note. We often leave our kindest tribute until it is too late.

"But there was a glory about it too. His death gave us courage. We forgot our fear. The Cross made the difference. It is the magnet that will one day draw all kinds of people to the Master.

"I believe. Jesus is the promised Messiah.

"He has changed my life. I have been born again—after I was old.

"What about you?"

9
Preaching in the Context of Crises

J. Altus Newell

Crisis literally means decision. It transliterates the Greek word krisis. In medical terminology, however, crisis has come to mean "a paroxysmal attack of pain, distress, or disordered function."[1] Thus, crisis is characterized by two major factors: the suddenness and severity of a malady or disfunction. The term denotes that rapid and radical complications have taken place.

In a broader sphere, crisis describes similarly sudden and severe complications in human circumstances. As such, crisis may be individual or collective. This presentation focuses on preaching in the context of collective, or congregational, crisis.

During the bitterly cold Saturday night of January 9, 1982, youthful burglars broke into the facilities of the Saint Matthews Baptist Church in Louisville, Kentucky. Before leaving, one of them set fire to a pile of solvent-soaked rags he placed in the church parlor. The fire spread undetected during the early morning hours of Sunday, January 10, until it literally exploded through the sanctuary, offices, and fellowship areas of the church. A major portion of the church's facilities were destroyed. Suddenly and severely, that congregation was plunged into crisis.

Such circumstances of collective crisis occur more frequently than often is imagined. A vicious tornado slashes through a heavily populated area. A bus loaded with children headed toward a church camp overturns. A smoldering relational problem erupts publicly with shattering congregational consequences.

Biblically, historically, and experientially, Christian preaching sometimes must be done in the context of collective crisis. Effective preaching in such circumstances requires understanding both of the process of sudden congregational grief and of the potential of preaching as proactive response to facilitate grief-resolution.

I. The Process of Sudden Congregational Grief

In his book *Pastoral Care and Counseling in Grief and Separation*, Wayne Oates describes the psychophysiology of sudden, or acute, grief. In addition to the normative phases of anticipatory grief—denial, anger, bargaining, despair, and acceptance—acute grief involves immediate states of shock, panic, and numbness. About shock, Oates says, "the person reacts as if physically hit, stunned, by a blow with a heavy object."[2] Panic, Oates goes on to explain, is the correlate at the psychological level of the physiological state of shock. According to Jurgen Reusch in the book *Therapeutic Communication*, "management of a situation in which panic develops is dependent upon the emergence of a leader."[3]

The third factor in sudden grief—numbness—usually occurs after the initial shock and panic subside. Persons, Oates says, may "complain of not being able to feel, of not feeling close to people or to God, of not knowing how to respond."[4] Following these states of shock, panic, and numbness, other more normative grief feelings return.

II. Proactive Response to Sudden Grief Through Preaching and Worship

A therapeutic program of preaching in response to congregational crisis should be based on authentic biblical principles of grief resolution. In the little monograph *Life's Detours*, Wayne Oates offers five such principles. They are <u>fellowship</u>, <u>perspective</u>, <u>realism</u>, <u>compensation</u>, and <u>resurrection</u>.[5] Each of these principles proved to be valid and helpful during the crisis at Saint Matthews Baptist Church.

<u>Fellowship</u>. This need is for true Christian <u>koinonia</u>, the sharing and bearing of mutual burdens, rather than for the superficial frivolity that often is mistaken for fellowship. At Saint Matthews, the decision was made to have a worship service on the Sunday morning while the fire was still being fought. This decision was more

instinctive and emotional than rational. But it proved to be the single most important factor in launching grief resolution. Nearly 1,100 persons gathered in the graciously offered chapel of nearby Southern Baptist Theological Seminary. Three vital needs were met—the need to express grief in the midst of caring friends, the need to receive accurate information, and the need to reaffirm covenants with God and one another.

A correlate of the need for koinonia was the intense desire for and openness to leadership. The pastor becomes a vicarious symbol of crisis response. In such situations, Oates observed, "the pastor must exercise firm, clear leadership."

Perspective. A second principle of proactive response involves the need to gain perspective on the crisis. People needed the regular opportunity not only to cry together but also to laugh—to see "the ridiculous, the audacious, and the funny." Persons desired to latch onto a sense of hope. The watchword for recovery originated in one spontaneous pastoral remark, "The church facilities may have burned, but the church itself is alive and well!"

Realism. A third principle is the need to be kept in touch with reality. A considerable problem arose at this point within the Saint Matthews' congregation. Because of meeting at the seminary on Sunday mornings and in the facilities of a Presbyterian church at other times, much of the congregation had no contact with the site of the burned facilities. After several months, a few members began proposing that the church should arrange indefinite use of the borrowed facilities and forego a rebuilding program. As quickly as possible, the congregation returned to the remaining church facilities for Sunday night and weekday activities. This return brought a corresponding return to reality regarding the need for rebuilding.

Compensation. A fourth principle is based on the physiological reality that "when one part of the body is removed, such as a kidney, a lung, or an eye, the other companion of that part tends to strengthen and take over the functions of the lost part." The surprising experience at Saint Matthews was that, because of the crisis, many people felt more needed by the church and were more disposed to give themselves unselfishly to the church's mission.

Throughout the congregation, there was heightened sensitivity and response to the crisis needs of others.

Resurrection. This fifth principle of proactive response to crisis is perceived in the New Testament as the preeminent principle of Christian life—and that not just of some future life but of life here and now. Gradually, a resurrection perspective began to take hold in many members of the congregation—that the "fiery trial" was not an exit but an entrance; not a dead end but a doorway into a new chapter of life given by the grace of God.

III. A Program for Preaching in Response to Congregational Crisis

The program of preaching developed in the context of the Saint Matthews' crisis had four phases. Each sought to promote the principles of proactive response. The four phases dealt with: the nature and mission of the church faced with crisis, crisis response in the life of Christ, other biblical models for crisis response, and response to questions about the nature of God.

The Nature and Mission of the Church. During the weeks immediately following the fire, the primary goal in preaching was to reaffirm the nature of the church as the "called-out" people of God. Sermons during this period often utilized the imagery of the disaster itself. The messages included:

"The Church Triumphant Is Alive and Well" (Rom. 8)

"The Church's One Foundation" (Matt. 16:13-18)

"Building on the One Foundation" (1 Cor. 3:9-16)

The crisis gave an unparalleled opportunity to begin afresh in church planning. Providentially, a Strategic Planning Committee had been scheduled the week after the fire to begin indepth evaluation of the church program. This committee utilized SBC Long Range Planning materials to guide the church in proactive response—first, by defining the church's purpose and objectives. Preaching was coordinated with the work of this committee. A series of messages was preached under the title, "The Church's Mission"— the Mission of Worship, the Mission of Witness, the Mission of Education, and the Mission of Ministry.

The Response to Crisis in the Life of Christ. A second phase of preaching consisted of Lenten messages communicating the dynamics of crisis response in the life of Christ. These messages dealt sequentially with:

• the temptation to deny difficulty and to avoid suffering. The message drawn from the Gethsemane experience was entitled "Dealing Directly with Difficulty";

• the redemptive nature of what Paul called "The Fellowship of His Sufferings." The church's solidarity with all those who suffer was the emphasis;

• the "death experiences" we encounter throughout life. The "Reality of Resurrection" is that these death experiences do not spell disaster because of the power of God at work in Jesus. They are not exits, but entrances into more life than we could have imagined.

Other Biblical Models for Crisis Response. A third phase of preaching sought other biblical models for crisis response. The messages included:

"Trusting the God Who Acts"—Elijah
"Living by Open Windows"—Daniel
"Growing Hearts in a Groping World"—Jonah
"Venturing Toward Victory"—Abraham
"The Passover People"—Moses

Questions About the Nature of God. A fourth phase of preaching found a natural place as the immediate impact of the crisis waned. This series probed questions about the nature of God in the face of evil and suffering. The series was entitled "Questions You Always Wanted to Ask About God." Individual topics included:

"Does God Go After People?" (Ps. 139)
"Does God Sometimes Seem Silent?" (Hab. 1—2)
"Why Doesn't God Do Something About Evil?" (Matt. 13:24-30)
"Where Is God in the Midst of Change?" (Heb. 12:25-29)
"Can God Really Be Trusted?" (Gen. 3; Rom. 8)

The Importance of Worship. Evaluation of the congregation regarding the ministries which meant the most during the crisis experience showed that the major source of help and strength was the worship services. Alongside preaching, choral presentations and the celebration of the Lord's Supper were vital sources of meaning.

Personal and congregational prayer experiences encouraged people to speak <u>with</u> God about our need. Hymns of praise voiced faith and hope. "How Firm a Foundation" became the theme song of the church for the period of recovery.

> When thro' fiery trials thy pathway shall lie,
> My grace, all-sufficient, shall be thy supply;
> The flame shall not hurt three; I only design
> Thy dross to consume, and thy gold to refine.[6]

IV. Some Lessons for the Preacher from the Experience of Congregational Crisis

In the Chinese language, the word for <u>crisis</u> is composed of two characters—one means "danger," the other, "opportunity." The experience of congregational crisis is a dangerous opportunity in which there are <u>problems</u> to expect and <u>potential</u> to explore.

<u>Problems to Expect.</u> The most severe problem I encountered as pastor was that I was experiencing great loss and grief at the same time as my congregation—the loss of my library and other personal possessions in my study, as well as the loss of a cherished place to preach and worship. At the time, it seemed crucial to respond to the emergency needs of the congregation rather than to my own needs. However, after two months of a continual schedule of emergency meetings and measures, I was depleted, exhausted, and my body rebelled. Fortunately, a short period of tests and rest brought a return to health and to the reality of my own grief-work.

Another potential problem for the preacher in a physical disaster is the loss of his pastoral records and notes. Fortunately, I had taken advice several years before to keep copies of sermon notes and manuscripts in two places. Thus, while my seminary and preaching resource files were lost, as well as my books, sermon notes were preserved in files at my home.

A third problem area involved the church's insurance program. A program of "replacement value" insurance had been instituted three years prior to the fire. Otherwise, the facilities likely would have been insured only for sixty percent of their value. Loopholes soon became apparent, however, even in the "replacement value" coverage. An insurance rider was needed to cover the full value of ministers' libraries, which are considered personal property and are covered for only a token amount under standard policies.

Potential to Explore. The danger of crisis is more than matched by the potential for Christian preaching in the context of crisis. One area of potential is the unusual openness of persons in collective crisis to hear and heed the Word of God. The radical shake-up of human circumstances brings an earnestness and urgency to the reception of the preaching event.

A second area of potential is the opportunity to reevaluate church objectives and programming. This area may be the most influential source of progress for the church in the long run. Such a major disruption makes possible the planning of change in which dross truly can be consumed and gold refined.

A third area of potential is the development of greater individual and congregational maturity through "the fellowship of suffering." As Romans 5:3-5 puts it: "More than that, we rejoice in our sufferings, knowing that suffering produces endurance, and endurance produces character, and character produces hope, and hope does not disappoint us" (RSV).

While the context of crisis is not to be sought, it is the dangerous opportunity in which the voice of faith can say, "I want you to know, brethren, that what has happened to me has really served to advance the gospel" (Phil. 1:12, RSV).

Notes

1. *Webster's Seventh New Collegiate Dictionary* (Springfield, Massachusetts: G. and C. Merriam Company, 1970).

2. Wayne E. Oates, *Pastoral Care and Counseling in Grief and Separation* (Philadelphia: Fortress Press, 1976), p. 37.

3. Quoted by Oates, *Pastoral Care and Counseling in Grief and Separation,* p. 37.

4. Ibid., p. 39.

5. Wayne E. Oates, *Life's Detours* (Nashville: The Upper Room, 1974), pp. 13-21.

6. John Rippon's *Selection of Hymns,* 1787.

Thy Will Be Done
Matthew 26:36-42

What do we mean when we pray, "Thy will be done"? There is perhaps no subject about which more confusion exists, and no subject about which we need to think more clearly, than the subject of "the will of God."

For instance, a dearly loved member of a family dies after a lengthy illness. The family says, "Well, we must accept it. It is the will of God." But for weeks, that family has spared no expense seeing that their loved one received the finest medical care. They called in the best specialists. They utilized all the advances of medical technology. By every means at their disposal, they fought against a dread disease.

Were they all that time fighting against the will of God? If their loved one had recovered, would they not have called the recovery the will of God? Can recovery and death equally be God's intention?

Or take other examples. A young couple is elated with the birth of their first child. They learn on the second day that the infant has cystic fibrosis. Another family member piously counsels them, "Well, it is tragic. But remember, it would not have happened if it were not the will of God." Does God cause the suffering of innocent children?

A Christian family is awakened by a telephone call in the middle of the night. It's the sheriff of the county where their daughter is attending university. "I regret to have to tell you," the sheriff says, "your daughter has been killed in an automobile accident." The mother still believes that God chose to take her daughter from her. Did God choose that?

A politician with lots of savvy and even more knavery gets by with all kinds of shady deals. His political clout increases so much that he reaches national prominence. At a religious meeting, he attributes his success to God. Is his success really the result of the will of God?

How in the world can the will of God be reconciled with heartbreaking divorces, cruel suffering, deformed children, natural disasters?

How many people simply don't try to reconcile them. For some, this is their reason for not believing in God or at least not believing in a good God.

Albert Camus, the French Nobel Prize winner for literature, put his belief in the mouth of one of his characters. In Camus's book *The Plague*, a doctor trying to minister in the midst of an epidemic says, "I refuse to believe in a God who lets innocent children suffer."[1]

What do you mean when you pray, "Father, . . . thy will be done"?

In the midst of the battle for Britain during World War II, Dr. Leslie Weatherhead preached a series of messages on this subject to his congregation at London's City Temple. The messages are so incisive and helpful that they still are being published.[2] Weatherhead said that the subject of "the will of God" must be divided into three parts: the intentional will of God, the circumstantial or permissive will of God, and the ultimate or, what I prefer to call, the redemptive will of God. "The trouble arises," Weatherhead said, "because we use the phrase 'the will of God' to cover all three (parts) without making any distinctions between them."[3]

Look with me today at this subject, not as a matter of academic or theoretical interest but rather out of the real-life situation in which you and I have questioned or do question or will question the meaning of the will of God.

I. Consider first the intentional will of God. In Matthew 18:14, Jesus said: "It is not the will of my Father who is in heaven that one of these little ones should perish" (RSV). If you ever need something to hold onto when all else seems to be slipping, remember this verse of Scripture and the One who said it.

Jesus believed that God has an intention for all of his creation. This intention is not in any way evil. Instead, it is in every way good. God's intention is that his creation might come to fulfillment.

The whole Bible is the record of God putting his good intention in front of his highest creation. God's intentional will is recorded in his Word. It is characterized in the Sermon on the Mount, in which the law and prophets are said to be fulfilled. It is characterized in the double commandment of love which even for Paul is "the fulfilling of the law." It is characterized in the full biblical revelation of how God intends us to live. For us to pray "Thy will be done" is to pray first, "God, bring your intention about <u>in</u> me and <u>through</u> me."

Unfortunately, the Greek language obscures the colorful, concrete Aramaic behind this petition. What the Greek translates doing "the will of God" means literally to do "what is well-pleasing to God," even, to do "God's pleasure."[4] But don't make the mistake of thinking that what is involved here is fulfilling particular commandments or rules which can be counted up afterwards.

The phrase "doing what is well-pleasing to God" is a phrase of family relationship. It indicates a positive responsiveness between a child and a father. That is why Jesus said, "Unless you turn and become like children, you will never enter the kingdom of heaven" (Matt. 18:3). God already has revealed his intention for his children. When you and I pray "Thy will be done," we do not have to wonder what is meant about God's intention. It is that we his children do "what is well-pleasing to him."

Our response can be like the last words of Richard Baxter, the English Puritan, of whom it was said, "He preached as a dying man to dying men, and never sure to preach again." Baxter's last words were, "Lord, what Thou wilt, where Thou wilt, and when Thou wilt."[5]

II. <u>In considering the will of God, we must reckon also with God's circumstantial or permissive will</u>. The first testimony of Scripture is that, "In the beginning God created the heavens and the earth. . . . And God saw everything that he had made, and behold, it was very good" (Gen. 1:1,31, RSV). If Scripture stopped there, we would have no problem with the will of God. But that is not all the Bible says.

The Bible witnesses to God's permission of circumstantial freedom within his creation. God has made room for events to happen, for choices to be made, for circumstances to occur. Genesis says that

God did this so that he could enjoy relationship with his creation and particularly with his highest creation.

God created man and woman not as puppets or robots. Instead, God bestowed upon human beings a matchless gift—the gift of freedom in decision making. He wanted man and woman to choose to respond to him, to want to share with him in meaningful relationship.

The Bible witnesses that God permits the choices of human beings to have a real effect. If I reach out and hit you, God allows my decision to have a real effect. Is God responsible for my decision? Not in the sense of intending that I hurt you, but only in the sense of creating a world in which freedom and circumstance are permitted.

Likewise, God permits the circumstance of the natural universe to have a real effect. Creation has within it natural processes and principles, which usually are predictable and which it is the province of science to trace.

The law of gravitation is one such principle. A rock tossed off a cliff will plunge downward until it strikes the ground—and so will an airliner, filled with people, if that airliner loses power. God permits predictable and unpredictable natural circumstances. If we take freedom seriously, we must say that some things happen because God permits them.

But beyond this, the Bible witnesses that there is a power of rebellion against God in this universe. It can be seen in creation, in human community, and inside human beings. The Bible speaks of this demonic force in personal terms. The Bible calls the leader of this power Satan.

The power of God is stronger than this power of evil. The decisive battle has been fought. But this adversary of God has not yet been totally subdued. Evil is still part of the circumstances of the universe.

The Bible witnesses then in all these ways to circumstances which occur not because of God's direct intention but because of God's permission.

If this were all we knew about God, I would have no basis for asking you to believe in the goodness of God and of his will for human beings. If revelation stopped here, then persons would have ample reason to justify blaming God for what he permits. But revelation does not stop here!

III. We must look finally at the ultimate or, more precisely, the redemptive will of God. This is the most important message God has ever given. Let's face it: we live in an unstable and often cruel world—a world where innocence is not safe, where beauty often is defaced, where truth gets twisted, where good people have terrible things happen to them, and where many of the most undeserving have to suffer unbelievably.

It is right there that God's greatest message meets you and me, right at the tomb of tragedy, right at the point where we understand the difficulty and pain and loss at the heart of human life, right at the point where we are tempted to move toward self-pity or hostility or despair.

The message is that God does not evade tragedy or overlook tragedy. Rather, God meets tragedy head-on and transforms it. God is at work to redeem this world, our lives, and our circumstances.

Romans 8:28 is a Scripture verse most of us know by heart. You may have grown up quoting it, as I did, the way it's rendered in the King James Version of the Bible. It says: "We know that all things work together for good to them that love God, to them who are the called according to his purpose."

According to that translation, "all things work together for good." And how often a minister hears this—in a hospital or a funeral home or wherever persons are involved in tragedy. "Everything that happens, happens for a purpose," people say. "We may not see the purpose or understand why, but God knows why. Thus, we have to endure tragedy and accept it," they say, "because everything is happening for a purpose." I've heard people say that piously or bravely on the outside, while they were being torn apart on the inside.

If you've had difficulty with that interpretation, then I have good news for you. The King James Version at this point does not reflect the oldest manuscripts. In these Romans 8:28 says, "In all things, God is working for good with those who love him."

According to Romans 8:28, it is not Christian or scriptural to have to say that everything that happens is sent by God. That belief was propounded by the early Stoics, not the early Christians. Does God will for the little baby to die? Does God will for millions to suffer malnutrition and starvation? Does God want the airliner to crash? Did God mean for that father to lose his job and his family to be destitute? Does God intend for there to be war and murder and hatred and hurt of human beings?

As your pastor, I must tell you that based on all I've been able to discover about God, I must answer, "No, a thousand times no." God does not intentionally will everything that happens. Romans 8:28 does not say, "All things work together for good." Rather it says, "In everything <u>God</u> works for good with those who love him." This is God's ultimate, redemptive will.

And right here, I believe, is the secret to praying "Thy will be done." It is the secret Jesus knew in Gethsemane. When Jesus prayed there, he was well aware that suffering was ahead of him. He could have chosen not to suffer. But Jesus chose to trust God in the suffering and to hope beyond the suffering. He did this because he lived out what Paul later expressed in Romans 8:28. God does not cause everything that happens, but God can take what happens, even the worst that happens, and can bring good from it.

The last hours of Jesus Christ were filled with pain as any one of us might ever face. That was human tragedy of the most intense sort. The Man of loving joy was ruthlessly cut down by hostility and destructiveness. If ever there were more undeserved suffering, I don't know where it is.

Yet, God took that awful event of crucifixion and worked to transform it. Through his power, the death of Jesus became the instrument of redemption. The very persons who committed that awful crime found that, in the Cross and resurrection, their sin was forgiven.

What happened to Jesus reveals the nature of God and his ultimate, redemptive purpose for our lives. He is the God who is able to take the worst that has ever happened and bring good from it, if we trust him as Jesus did.

Ella Wheeler Wilcox has written these lines entitled "Gethsemane."

> All those who journey, soon or late,
> Must pass within the garden's gate;
> Must kneel alone in darkness there,
> And battle with some fierce despair.
> God pity those who cannot say:
> "Not mine but Thine"; who only pray:
> "Let this cup pass," and cannot see
> The purpose in Gethsemane.[6]

What about the will of God? Do we recognize God's intention for our lives and all creation? Do we acknowledge God's permission of circumstantial freedom? Do we trust God's redemption in the midst of life's tragedies? If so, then we can pray as Jesus taught us, "Father, . . Thy will be done" (Matt. 6:9).

Notes

1. Albert Camus, *The Plague,* trans. Stuart Gilbert (New York: Alfred A. Knopf, 1948), p. 18.

2. Leslie D. Weatherhead, *The Will of God* (Nashville: Abingdon Press, 1944).

3. Ibid., pp. 11-12.

4. Ernest Lohmeyer, *"Our Father": an Introduction to the Lord's Prayer,* trans. John Bowden (New York: Harper & Row, 1965), p. 119.

5. Quoted by Clarence Macartney, *The Lord's Prayer* (New York: Fleming H. Revell, 1942), p. 38.

6. Ella Wheeler Wilcox, "Gethsemane," *Poems of Power* (Chicago: Albert Whitman, 1901).

10

Preaching in the Context of Worship

Robert W. Bailey

English theologian J. S. Whale captured the attitude of many contemporary church people as he wrote:

> Instead of putting off our shoes from our feet because the place where we stand is holy ground, we are taking nice photographs of the burning bush from suitable angles; we are chatting about theories of Atonement with our feet on the mantlepiece, instead of kneeling down before the wounds of Christ.[1]

Almost half of the American population views the Sunday morning worship hour as an accepted tradition. Each of us here has been deeply entrenched in Sunday morning worship for decades—perhaps all of our lives. However, our proximity to the altar does not necessarily equate our nearness to the throne of grace, our interest in the direction of God, or our responsiveness to the heart of God. We in the Christian church have been on the verge of greatness and power so often, and yet most frequently we have turned our backs before we ever saw the face of God. We have long sensed the need for renewal in the church, and we have observed that most churches have chosen to go the route of lay renewal, prayer groups, small group work, or baptism of the Holy Spirit.

Few of us have consistently recognized the vital aspect of worship. Few of us have identified the crucial need of the renewal of worship. Few of us have emphasized the vital truth that the Christian faith will wither and die unless it is sustained by living encounters with the one true God.[2]

It is both awesome and frightening to realize that we of all people find it easier to talk about the atonement than to kneel before our

179

Lord and our God! Unless we proclaimers are willing to face the wounds of Christ and realize afresh what he has done for us, we shall never bring those whom god has called us to lead into a life-changing relationship with Jesus Christ. When we realize the depth and price of God's love in Christ, we must either do something or turn and walk away!

Typical Preaching in the Context of Worship

In order to help us focus on our personal stance, we need to ferret out just what is the typical preaching in the context of worship. Almost every thoughtful writer on the subject has indicted the attitude of the Protestant preacher which has traditionally viewed the hymns and anthems, prayers, Scripture reading, and offering as "preliminaries" for the main event—the sermon! Even baptism and Communion are usually viewed as appendages to the primary trunk of worship either by a sheer accident in the church calendar or by the choice of the pastor. In an untold number of churches Communion is tacked on at the end of the worship hour, often beginning after 12:00.[3] We have followed denominational language and expectation for so long that either we use or we endorse the attitude of our teachers and members who refer to going to "big church" or "staying for preaching."

A great number of pastors have relied on some type of sensationalism to prop up the interest of their congregations. Some do it through entertaining sermons. Some do it through spectacular music. Some do it through a stream of guest speakers. Some do it through programmed enthusiasm. Some do it through a splash of colors and lights. At the base of all the sensationalism has been a marked effort to manipulate people and no effort to nurture people closer to God.

Perhaps not all of the typical preaching in the context of worship has been intentionally shallow and deceiving. Quite honestly, it appears that many seminaries and even more churches have not always had high expectations for the preaching or worship being done. Consider the last half century. There have been times in which the training and expectation were focused on theology without any stress on verbal skills, poetic conceptualization, or innovative worship. For the most part, this breed of preacher has been fluent in theological language but stammering as a preacher and worship leader.

Again, there have been times when the training and expectation were focused on the practical dimensions of ministry without any requirements of preaching or any skills in worship leadership. In the name of being "practical," some of the seminaries offered not a single course on worship, though the music school devoted part of the time in an interdisciplinary course to the importance of worship. For the most part this breed of preacher has been knowledgeable in pastoral care, aware of social issues, but halting as a preacher and worship leader.

We cannot expect good preaching and sound worship leadership when there is no study or training expected or required in preaching and worship. And yet with no training, we have expected stimulating preaching and worship! On the other hand, we have anticipated excitement and responsiveness in worship when we have rigidly clung to the same forms of worship. This is true both in those churches who have no printed order of worship as well as those who do print it. Some churches have gone year after year, decade after decade, pastor after pastor, singing the same responses in the same place, hearing the same prayers in the same place, listening to the same announcements in the same place, and then both the clergy and the laity have dared question at times why the attendance has declined and fewer young people have come. We are deceiving ourselves if we think that worship can be so repetitiously constructed that people can sleep their way through it without missing anything and still be inspired by what takes place! While the worship form must never become the object of worship, it is important that the freshness and vitality of worship be presented in a dynamic way so that the people will desire and expect to encounter the living God.

A critical key in the whole matter of worship is the worship leader, the pastor. It is hard for people to rise above their leader. It is perhaps impossible for worshipers to draw closer to God in the worship experience than the pastor is. It is hard for people to grasp a vision their leader does not see. It is perhaps impossible for worshipers to feel that each worship experience is a new event for hearing and responding to God when their pastor repeats himself. It is hard for people to move beyond their leader. It is perhaps impossible for worshipers to engage their lives in a dynamic, transforming experience with God when their pastor is unprepared. It is hard for people to climb above their leader. It is perhaps impossible for worshipers to see the transition of stimulating worship to changed living when their pastor demonstrates no expectancy or change himself.

Tedious Problems in Renewing Worship

Perhaps without further belaboring of the point, we can acknowledge the weaknesses of the typical preaching in the context of worship. We have teetered at this point for several decades, and many have fallen off due to the tedious problems in renewing worship.

> The cover is off! Pandora's box is open! The worship of the church will never be the same! Multimedia shows, jazz masses, rock songs, balloons and placards, 'groovy' language, 'flicks,' and changing lights are here![4]

is the way one person described the crisis in worship during the last decade. In an effort to correct the flaws in previous worship forms, the pendulum has often swung to the other extreme so that "the line between what is done in church and what might be done at a demonstration on a social issue is erased."[5] And in the elimination of the distinctiveness of Christian worship, often the laity have lost the landmarks which guided them through the maze of waste and dread into the glory of God's presence.

For a number of years pastors who have been living in panic over the decline of their churches have embraced the "of course" movement. That is, at any point change in worship is mentioned, their response is "of course" without giving any careful consideration of how to review the revised worship to see if it will stand the test of authentic biblical worship. Until recent years almost all the stress was on doing worship in the "traditional," "proper" manner. Now more and more leaders are backing off and allowing—or even encouraging—members to "do their own thing" in worship. Some pastors have already left the churches where they initiated or allowed the "of course" movement to take root. Other pastors are still feeling the pain inflicted by troubled worshipers on both extremes—those who want more change at their demand and those who are upset by change seemingly for the sake of change. It appears that simultaneously the crisis in the authority of the pastor has linked with the crisis in the meaning of worship. The result is that some pastors have lost a grip on the worship in their churches all the while they have sought to please the aggressive verbal people who have demanded that things no longer be the way they have always been.

Sunday morning worship has been viewed by many as the deadest hour of the week. A great number of people get up on Sunday morning and go to the church building out of habit. They sit there semiconscious for an hour, only passively reacting to what is being said and done. Karl Barth declared that Christians go to church to make their last stand—against God! Instead of worship being viewed as an opportunity to encounter God, it has been seen in the past as a time to promote and prop up the church and now as a time to parade the likes and skills of the innovative performers! Clearly when there is a problem with anything, there is the grave possibility of overreacting and missing the target we intended to hit.

Jonathan Swift captured the real feeling of Martin Luther in the little story "A Tale of a Tub." This tale describes three men. Martin, repentant for having embellished the coat his father gave him with clear directions to keep it plain, removed some of the gaudier frills while his brother Jack, who represented Calvin, removed with great enthusiasm every attachment from his coat; and at the same time his brother Peter, who represented the Pope, busied himself gathering up anything and everything Martin and Jack cast off and added it to his heavily decorated coat. Luther's original intent seemingly was not to leave the Catholic Church or to strip it of its liturgy. Rather, he desired to reinvest the liturgy with a renewed centrality and dominance of the Word, the Spirit of God, the inspired Word which was especially active in the preached Word rooted in a sound text from the Scripture.[6] The end result was quite different from what Luther originally intended. And in a similar vein, the end result of a great deal of the worship renewal of the last two decades is quite different from the original intention!

Cleland's classic definition of faulty preaching said:

> Preaching has become a byeword for long and dull conversation of any kind; and whoever wishes to imply, in any piece of writing, the absence of everything agreeable and inviting, calls it a sermon.[7]

This is a far cry from the view of preaching as "a manifestation of the Incarnate Word from the Written Word by the Spoken Word."[8] Some significant changes in preaching in the context of worship are needed, but we have seldom gone about it the right way in our hasty efforts to renew worship and satisfy our churches.

One sobering reminder of the need for change was the continual growth of the sermon in the eighteenth and nineteenth centuries. As Killinger describes the increasingly lengthy sermon, it was like "the legendary camel which kept drinking water and expanding until she had filled her owner's tent and had finally crowded everybody else off the oasis."[9]

This use of the sermon has been regrettable and has left side effects that will not quickly be remedied or eliminated. But at the same time we have too readily distorted the focus of preaching, lost the emphasis of worship, recklessly shifted to human problems, mistakenly lost the divine dimension, carelessly confused the laity, and indifferently turned off the worshipers. There must be some corrective course of action whereby a tenable proposal for a union of preaching and worship could be achieved.

At the outset we must restore the thrust of God-centered worship.

> Worship, simply put, is the acknowledgment of God's supreme worth. We worship God because of who he is, not because of what he can do for us. We worship not to glorify ourselves but to celebrate God's majesty. We do not worship to build up our church, its program, or

even God's kingdom. We worship to affirm what God has done, what God is doing, and what God will do. Contrary to what some may believe or say, worship is an obligation, not an option, for the Christian. Worship is not always easy. It always requires disciplined effort.[10]

William Temple said to worship is . . .

> to quicken the conscience of the holiness of God,
> to feed the mind with the truth of God,
> to purge the imagination by the beauty of God,
> to open the heart to the love of God,
> to devote the will to the purpose of God.

All this is gathered up in that emotion which most cleanses us from selfishness because it is the most selfless of all emotions—adoration.[11]

Authentic worship is directed not toward any person, organization, or cause but toward God.

> We honor <u>God</u>. We praise <u>God</u>. We adore <u>God</u>. We obey <u>God</u>. We praise <u>God</u> above all the earth. . . . Through worship we gain a vision of God. We interpret life and work under God, and we dedicate life to God. We give our tribute to God in worship, acknowledging his holiness and providence. In worship, we remember God's mighty acts in our behalf, affirm our faith, and celebrate God's grace in making us persons of worth, able to come before him.[12]

Just as worship must be God-centered, it must be viewed as an event, a happening, a celebration, an occurrence, an encounter. Worship is not a passive spectator sport but a dynamic interaction between the Creator God and the created person through the grace of the Lord Jesus and the presence of the Holy Spirit!

In a similar vein, preaching is an event which must be biblically based. In 1968 William L. Malcomson wrote a book entitled *The Preaching Event* in which he said that preaching is a "communication event" in which the elements are the congregation, the preacher, and the message.[13] Cleland said preaching, like the rest of worship, is a combined effort of both clergy and laity. Preaching thus is personal encounter in which the pastor and people gain shared meaning.

Preaching has been defined as "the event in which the biblical text is interpreted in order that its meaning will come to expression in the concrete situation of the hearers."[14] This style of preaching can strengthen worship which prompts an inner movement toward God. True worship is never simply an intellectual concept, head knowledge, or even social activity. Worship is the celebration of God and who he is, and the worship event allows us to enter into this celebration and thereby encounter God uniquely.

> Worship involves all of life and a specific act in a definite place. Christian worship is not authentic without a specific encounter with God that produces definite obedience to God. Worship is a response to God's revelation in Christ. Worship is inspired by gratitude and rooted in the historical Christian heritage. Worship is an experience in which worshipers need guidance and time to speak and listen. Worship is a giving to and a receiving from God. Worship affects one's thought and one's feelings, necessitating a clear head and a warm heart. Indeed, worship involves the whole person! The religious emotions of worship include wonder, gratitude, fear, reverence, and baffling mystery. Corporate worship is a congregational event.[15]

We must constantly work to prevent worship's degeneration into nothing other than a performance alternating between the prompters—the preacher and choir!

Quite frankly, we must work simultaneously on preaching and worship. We cannot drop one for the other and maintain the strength needed. We cannot major on one without the other and have the balance needed. We cannot emphasize one without the other and have the truth required. It takes conscious, consistent work to insure that our preaching is not trite, shallow, flashy, manipulative, self-advancing, or program-bound. Similarly we must work regularly on worship so that it is not stiff, lifeless, forced, shabby, self-elevating, or church promoting. Preaching and worship must be sound and authentic, for the worship experience will be flat unless there is strength and vitality in both.

In his work *The Integrity of Preaching*, John Knox made the connection between preaching and worship so clearly and emphatically:

> Unless we conceive of preaching as being itself an act of worship, we miss what is most essential in it and what distinguishes it most radically from other kinds of teaching, religious or secular. The real truth of the matter is not that preaching merely happens usually to be set in a context of worship or that it is most effective when it has that kind of setting. Rather, it cannot be really preaching except in that context. If the context of worship is not there already, the true sermon creates it. Either preaching contributes to, provides a medium of, worship, or it is not preaching at all.[16]

In the best sense of the word, preaching is an offering made to God on behalf of the preacher. When the proclaimer comes with this attitude and with proper preparation, he is able simultaneously to speak to the congregation on behalf of God and to speak for the congregation in the presence of God. All of the elements of worship are bound up in the preaching event—adoration, thanksgiving, commitment, confession, seeking forgiveness, and intercession. When properly conceived, planned, prepared, and embodied, preaching and worship are interwoven and interpret each other.

Possibly the point where preaching and worship touch each other most dramatically are when they unite in a single effort to bring people to God so they will be moved to respond in loving service to man. Some critics of worship and writers about worship contend that there should not be a central theme of worship. They contest that the liturgy should be usual, traditional, unchanging, and only the sermon should be altered from Sunday to Sunday. While it is essential that the worship event should never be manipulated to promote a cause or elevate a person, there are no biblical or theological reasons why the preaching and worship should not focus on a single point. Indeed, it seems that when the worship event is shaped around a single theme the worshipers have a greater potential of entering into the experience and sensing a new dimension in which God is seeking to encounter them.

It appears that a balance has not been struck between ritual sameness and unnerving change in worship. As a result, many back away from the radical change by clinging to the traditional, comfortable, and customary forms of worship. The balance which can and must be held in tension is the dynamic preaching event which is cast within a dynamic worship event.

Two significant things can be done which will greatly enliven and stimulate the union of preaching and worship. The first is to plan ways for the participation of the worshipers other than as hymn singers or passive listeners. In my S.T.D. dissertation, I researched the difference lay participation makes in the preaching event.[17] In a project with John Claypool at Crescent Hill, I validated my thesis that the more actively involved worshipers are in the preaching event the more they perceive and retain. During the last dozen years, I have continued to work on this same principle.

For those of us accustomed to Southern Baptist worship forms, we have seldom moved beyond the responsive readings in the back of the hymnal. However, we should not be timid about working on the entire worship event with a view to how we can increase congregational involvement. Once we open our eyes to the possibilities, we can see multitudes of ways, times, and places to lead our people to the throne of grace in a more active manner than in the past. Some of the wide range of variables include

- a unison Scripture reading
- a responsive call to worship
- a corporate offertory response
- a unison summons to worship
- a responsive Scripture reading
- a corporate statement of belief
- a unison benediction
- a responsive offertory prayer
- a litany of thanksgiving
- a corporate summons to prayer
- a responsive benediction
- a corporate invocation
- a unison statement of faith.[18]

There are additional ways for spoken worship involvement, but you see the point that we can do more than a responsive reading from the back of the hymnal.

When you enable the worshipers to have a spoken part in the worship, you accomplish several important things. They feel affirmed by the worship leader. Their attention is heightened. They can voice some of their feelings, thoughts, questions, joys, concerns, and sins. They are encouraged by others who join them. They perceive that worship is an act not a show. In each of these and other ways you contribute something vital to the worshipers by having them to participate verbally in the worship event.

Just as spoken elements can be written and printed in the order of worship allowing the people to speak other than a responsive reading from the hymnal, likewise you can do more with music than just sing hymns.

A corporate musical meditation, musical call to prayer, musical call to worship, corporate musical benediction, congregational musical offertory, and congregational part in an anthem are but a few of the ways in which you can involve the congregation musically beyond hymn singing.[19]

I stated there are two ways of involving worshipers. Clearly the first is planning. This includes planning with your musicians, staff, and lay worship leaders. The second way is to provide some variety within the overall normal framework of the worship event. For example, it is not necessary for the people to pray in unison the Lord's Prayer every Sunday. Indeed, if they do so over a period of years, they will be spouting out words by rote; and the prayer will no longer have any personal meaning or spiritual significance for them. The choir's music need not appear at the same point in the worship each Sunday. One week you might plan a spoken call to worship and another week a responsive benediction. One week you might sing a response to the offering, and another week you might sing a congregational call to prayer. The point is, there can be freshness and variety in worship without going to the extremes of rock music, placards, flashing lights, and multimedia presentations in lieu of the sermon.

By gradually leading a congregation to this approach to the worship event, there is no reason the worshipers could not have at least two opportunities a week to express themselves in worship beyond the customary hymns. Each week those occasions can be altered.

Killinger makes a statement in his chapter on "Preaching and Worship" which makes his point and mine.

> There is no substitute for preaching in worship. It provides the proclamatory thrust without which the church is never formed and worship is never made possible. It complements the creedal, poetic nature of the liturgy and keeps before men the absolute contemporaneity of the gospel, as of a Word made always present and personal to them under the pressure of their current life-situations. . . . It forbids mere ritualism and automatism in the service by continually inserting into worship the presence of a new and unique word, one which is never quite the same again when preached in another setting or published in a compendium of sermons. Above all, it provides better than anything else the necessary encounter between the lackadaisical worshiper and the intensity of Christ's lordship. It, of all the elements in the liturgy, is primary, for it and it alone is able to guarantee the success of Christian worship and the Christian sacraments.[30]

Killinger's point is an eloquent statement for the centrality of preaching, and I affirm the vital focal point of preaching. But at the same time, he makes my point that sameness in the worship event loses a sense of freshness, cuts off a feeling of being personal, smacks of ritualism, encourages halfheartedness, and spawns coolness and distance toward God.

A century ago when American preaching was at its heyday, it was said of Phillips Brooks that he dared his hearers to accept the divine power that would move them to a level where they had never lived before. In this day, we need preaching just as powerful that is cast in the setting of a dynamic worship event. Worship that has such power renews us.

Worship that transforms was evidenced in Berlin several years ago. A church's property had been divided by the iron curtain. The sanctuary was in East Berlin and the parsonage in West Berlin. The youth in the West decided to gather at the parsonage on Reformation Sunday and sing Luther's great hymn, "A Mighty Fortress Is

Our God." They hoped their Christian brothers and sisters on the Communist side might hear them and be uplifted to worship God also. The Christian youth in the Communist sector gathered at the same time on their side of the wall. Just before Luther's hymn was begun, the East Berlin youth began to sing an old Reformation hymn:

> I can't go on.
> No comfort here abideth,
> Life's burden weighs me down
> It is too much!
> I cannot find relief
> All comfort takes its leave!
> Have mercy on me, Lord!
> I can't go on!

Immediately the youth on the West side of the wall changed hymns and responsed with the second verse of that hymn:

> You can go on!
> God's help will soon be there.
> He'll turn you from your grief
> And give you peace.
> You just must keep on fighting.
> Our Lord too suffered in His stride.
> Go on with Him—He's on your side.
> You can go on!

The youth on the East sang the third stanza which reiterated their inability to go on, and then the youth on both sides of that wall topped with barbed wire and broken glass sang, the final verse in unison:

> You can go on!
> There soon will be an end.
> God reaches out His hand,
> Look here—His hand, to you!
> Ah, let us pray and pray.
> And He will send the day.
> His help will make us say,

To Him be praise,
He is our strength and stay.[21]

Surely this is preaching in the context of worship at its best—a corporate encounter with God that so fills us with joy, that so transforms us into a vibrant fellowship, that so empowers us with strength that we can go on loving and serving God!

We can go on!

Notes

1. J. S. Whale, *Christian Doctrine* (Cambridge: University Press, 1941), p. 152.

2. Robert Bailey, *New Ways in Christian Worship* (Nashville: Broadman Press, 1981), p. 13.

3. John Killinger, *The Centrality of Preaching* (Waco: Word, Inc., 1969), p. 38.

4. Henry E. Horn, *Worship in Crisis* (Philadelphia: Fortress Press, 1972), p. 3.

5. Ibid.

6. Killinger, pp. 42-43.

7. James T. Cleland, *Preaching to Be Understood* (Nashville: Abingdon Press, 1965), p. 108.

8. Thomas H. Keir, *The Word in Worship* (Oxford: Oxford University Press, 1962), p. 12.

9. Killinger, p. 38.

10. Bailey, p. 17.

11. William Temple, *The Hope of a New World* (London: The Macmillan Co., Ltd. 1942), p. 30.

12. Bailey, pp. 17-18.

13. William L. Malcomson, *The Preaching Event* (Washington: Westminster Press, 1968), p. 9.

14. David J. Randolph, *The Renewal of Preaching* (Philadelphia: Fortress Press, 1969), p. 1.

15. Bailey, p. 14.

16. John Knox, *The Integrity of Preaching*, p. 76.

17. Robert W. Bailey, "The Revitalization of the Preaching Event, with Emphasis upon Lay Participation," Unpublished S.T.D. dissertation, The Southern Baptist Theological Seminary, Louisville, Kentucky, 1970.

18. Bailey, *New Ways*, p. 30.

19. Ibid., pp. 30-31.

20. Killinger, p. 51.

21. Daniel Day Walker, *Enemy in the Pew?* (New York: Harper and Row Publishers, 1967), pp. 68-69.

The Emptiness of Wrong Expectations
Psalm 95:1-11; John 4:1-34

Michael Maloney was the bishop of New York, the most influential Catholic in America, according to the fictitious best-selling novel *Act of God.* The novelist wove a masterful plot around Michael. One element of the story was the sudden appearance of an old college friend, now archaeologist, who was almost ready to publish his findings on some bones which he claimed to be Jesus' bones. The other aspect of the novel was the selection of the successor to the dying pope. According to an influential friend in Rome, Michael was the logical choice for the next pope.

The archaeologist stayed in Michael's home when he returned from a long Mideast dig. The more he told Michael about his findings, the more worried Michael became that the world just might believe the insane idea that Jesus' bones had been found! And the more Michael thought about the impending election of the new pope, the more uneasy he became that this atheistic archaeologist living, working, and writing in the basement of his house could jeopardize his chances of becoming pope. He concluded he must do something about his friend before his work was published.

The archaeologist was diabetic. One day Michael sent everyone away from the house except the busy archaeologist. He controlled the man's diet and caused him to have a diabetic attack. Michael did not give him any insulin. The man died as a direct result of Michael's action. Later while he was in Rome awaiting the election of the new pope, his niece's fiancé found the archaeologist's writings which Michael had hidden. The man threatened to expose Michael. The niece could not stand the truth ne. fiancé was going to reveal about her uncle's misdeeds, so she committed suicide. Michael returned

193

to New York for the funeral to learn later that another man had been chosen pope. He was an older, less able, but a more caring man than Michael.

Michael Maloney slid through a whole episode of wrong expectations, feeling that the salvation and future of Christ's church were totally dependent upon him. When it was all over, his friend was dead, his niece who was like a daughter was dead, he was still only bishop of New York, and he had to live with and seek to work through his guilt and grief. Michael's expectations had been all wrong, and he faced the rest of his life standing in the emptiness of his mistaken expectations.

The novelist ably captured the stance of many twentieth-century Americans. We are busy trying to manipulate the lives of others and even ourselves due to the mind-set of wrong expectations. Some of us are very pessimistic at this point in our nation's life and in world history. The discouraged people have a dismal outlook on life due to past disappointments and failures. Several years ago a popular singer recorded a song that described this view of life. The ballad-type song traced several disappointing events in the life of the singer. When her house burned, when she first saw a circus, and when her lover left her, she felt a sense of disappointment and emptiness. Things were not as she had expected them to be. When she acknowledged her emptiness, her friends asked why she did not end her life. Her reply was that she was not prepared for what would be her final disappointment because she knew that even when she faced death she would still be asking herself is this all there is. Pessimistic, despairing people try to fill their lives with many things and still wind up with sadness and unfulfilled expectations.

Another segment of society feels an intense sense of competition with others, and thus they push and shove to get their place before others pass them by. We see this struggle in the classroom, business, club, family, and even church, as people work frantically to stay "one up" on others whom they expect to try to undermine and surpass them. Several years ago nearly 100,000 people gathered at Riverfront Stadium in Cincinnati before a rock concert. The seats were not reserved. When the first door opened, the mob began to shove and push in order to get the best possible seats before others behind them did. The result of that sea of stampeding humanity was the death of eleven and the severe injury of others under the trampling feet of rushing people. Much to the amazement of outraged citizens and the families of those eleven, the management let the concert go on without acknowledging the tragedy. They did so because of their fear of what the crowd might have done if they had been forced to miss the concert. Their exit might have created an even greater misfortune.

Pessimism, suspicion, and self-driving concerns are all felt by many people today. Indeed, these feelings are often so great that they block the view of God which is held before us. The result is a simultaneous, cancerous attitude of self-preservation and self-worship.

Herod the Great was such a person. He was appointed governor of Judea by the Romans, and then he became the Jewish king. He maintained peace with an atrocious reign of terror. He was highly suspicious and paranoid of others and had people murdered for little or no reason at all. He eliminated by murder everyone he suspected was seeking to undercut him—including his wife, his mother, and three of his sons! This vengeance caused the Roman emperor, Augustus, to say, "It is safer to be Herod's pig than Herod's son."

To this pessimistic, suspicious figure, the Wise Men came seeking information about the newborn king (Matt. 2:1-9). In his monologue, Frederick Buechner says for the Wise Man,

> "Go and find me the child," the king told us, and as he spoke, his fingers trembled so that the emeralds rattled together like teeth. "Because I want to come and worship him," he said, and when he had said it, his hands were still as death. Death. I ask you, does a man need the stars to tell him that no king has ever yet bowed down to another king? He took us for children, that sly, lost old fox, and so it was like children that we answered him, "Yes, of course," we said, and went on our way. His hands fluttered to his throat like moths.[1]

Like so many people today, Herod wanted control over others whom he feared would hurt him or upset his scheme of things. And

Herod used the guise of religion to achieve his end. His response is so like those who feel threatened by someone, those who want someone else to "do religion" for them. He had no intention of worshiping! His vicious destruction of all male babies two years and younger was his retaliation when the Wise Men did not return to him and tell him where the young child—born over a year earlier—and his parents were living.

We have grown accustomed to identifying Herod's lack of desire to worship Christ, yet we so often fail to recognize the attitudes of our hearts today. A vital Christian woman declared that the last thing expected by most people when they come into the sanctuary is an encounter with God! If she is correct, what do people come to church expecting? Some feel put down in life, and they are expecting to find a way to rise to the top of the heap. Some expect religion to enable them to have some control and power over others. Some expect religion to solve all their problems. Some expect others to do the religious thinking and working for them, so all they have to do is on an occasional Sunday pick up a finished package they call "religion."

Herod was empty after his effort to secure his throne from a rival ruler. Likewise, any and all of us are empty when we expect to find meaningful life in any way other than actively seeking and encountering God in Jesus Christ. We are empty when we try to manipulate or destroy those whom we fear surpass us. We are empty when we turn our backs on God and pretend to be religious in order to be acceptable to those who are religious. We are empty when we expect our religion to dissolve all our problems and leave us free to do what we want to do in life.

Augustine an early Christian, said that man's chief purpose is to glorify God and enjoy him forever. Christ redeemed us and made us his own not just to save us from sin but so we could worship and serve him, so we could praise and love him. Our word worship comes from an older English word worthship, meaning that through adoration, word, and action we indicate the worth of someone or something we value. To worship God is to indicate that he is of most value in life, he is most important to us, he is supreme above all else. To worship God is to put him in first place, to give him our highest loyalty, to commit to him our total abilities, and to dedicate to him our greatest resources.

Our unquenchable thirst to worship God cannot be met in any false means we prescribe. Yet in our blindness toward God created by our wrong expectations, we often fail to see him and know him as he is. We create other gods and make gods of ourselves to no avail. A philosopher once said that the saddest moment in the life of an atheist comes when he feels thankful but has no God to whom he can express his thanks! We have a deep longing to worship God, but we can misuse and distort that need.

Standing by Jacob's Well in Samaria, Jesus encountered a woman with a dissipated reputation. In their conversation, he had disclosed her self-centeredness and asked her to go and bring her husband. Her response to this embarrassing question John recorded in the fourth chapter of his Gospel was to bring up a controversial religious issue (4:7-25). It is interesting to note that even today when we touch the fibers which unite people with God, people often try to sidestep us with a camouflage of religious controversy. The Samaritan woman mentioned the age-old issue of the Jewish-Samaritan separation and their different places of worship—Mount Gerizim in the North for Samaritans and Jerusalem in the South for the Jews. Jesus saw through all this religious pretense on the part of the woman and he dealt with her basic problem. He spoke words to her and to us today when he said it is not where but how one worships that is of ultimate importance. The real worship of God in spirit and in truth was not limited to the holy places of the Jews or the Samaritans. It could occur even at a wayside well!

Worship is the critical endeavor of deciding what is worthy in an ultimate sense, of energizing oneself by embracing what is most important. The act of worship is uniquely human. No other part of God's creation is capable of such discernment and self-commitment. Worship involves the multiple expressions, of awesomeness before God, of praising him, of giving thanks to him, of acknowledging him as Lord, of engaging him in love, of responding to him in obedience, and of serving him in all of life. Psalm 95 is one of the many settings in the Bible in which the urging to sing and celebrate in grateful praise before God is verbalized. Because he is both the Creator and the Good Shepherd, the people are directed to bow before him and heed his Word. The Psalm concludes with the sobering reminder that refusal to worship and follow God resulted in the forty-year wilderness wandering by the Hebrews. There are grave consequences to the emptiness of wrong expectations in our worship.

Between two and three thousand years ago when human knowledge of the earth and universe were so limited, the psalmist praised God for his greatness in creation. Today we know the closest star, the sun, is over 93,000,000 miles away and that there may be more than 100,000 stars in our galaxy! A figure that is staggering almost beyond imagination is that there may be more than 100,000 galaxies! And it takes more than 2,000,000 years for the light of some stars in our galaxy to reach the earth! How can we fail to stand in wonder and awe before the unmeasurable greatness of our God? He not only created us but also loves us and desires to have fellowship with us in worship. So long as we avoid worshiping the true and living God or so long as we make idols of ourselves or objects we possess, we will be buried in the pit of wrong expectations instead of bathing in the glory of the Almighty God.

If only we could learn from the experience of others and discover a new ray of light for our lives! Charles Dickens' dramatic novel *Great Expectations* captures the story of the development of a young man named Pip and offers us some hope for learning about our expectations. Pip was orphaned as a young boy and was reared in the home of his begrudging older sister. One day, while walking in the marsh country near his house, he encountered a wild-looking stranger who demanded Pip bring him food and a file to cut the iron chain from around his leg. Pip did both, and the man promised he would someday repay his kindness.

As Pip grew older, he received an offer to go to London to receive and education and become a gentleman. Pip expected all the time his benefactor was a wealthy maiden neighbor, Miss Haversham, who was preparing Pip to marry a girl she reared, Estella. Pip acquired his "great expectations" as he left his simple background and rose rapidly in society. But as he calculated his upward strides, Pip's moral values deteriorated at the same time his social graces improved. Pip fell from his high pinacle when Estella married his best friend, and Pip learned that his supporter was the criminal he had helped, not his wealthy neighbor. After a long illness during which Pip's brother-in-law nursed him, he abandoned his false expectations, returned to his original home, and accepted the limitations of his life. From what he learned, he was able to restore the virtue of his youth with the wisdom of his adulthood and make a reasonable life. Pip grew as a person and grew content with himself only when he was able to let go of wrong expectations and establish proper ones in their place.

In a way more graphic than this classic moral novel, Jesus Christ offers good news for our troubled day! There is hope for people with wrong expectations to be able to lay them aside and establish reasonable, proper expectations. Christ did not come to Israel to fulfill all their expectations of power and grandeur as a nation. And because he did not meet all their fond desires, Christ was rejected and crucified by the people. But now we can affirm that Christ came to reveal his Father, to call us into relationship, and to lead us to responsible discipleship.

We all long to be whole, yet most of us await some type of magical wizardry to transform us from what we are to what we should or want to be. We all want to have deep religious experiences, but the majority of us await someone else to figure out all the hard problems and then come tell us so we can worship too! We all want to grow up to be persons God created us to be, but most of the time we come back with some excuse for wrong expectations. We blame our sinfulness and weakness on parents and society, and we declare we will encounter God and become all he wants us to be when things get straightened out, when the pressures of life let up a little, when we have settled all our problems, when we have taken care of our family, or when we finally grow up. But so long as we expect to grow only after we have cared for all our problems and needs by ourselves, we will never move beyond our wrong expectations into the presence of the living God.

Each person's worship must include his or her own awareness of need or the attempt at worship is not genuine. Each person's worship must be a vital, personal experience, or it is nothing. Each person must be about the matter of encountering God today, or none of the days will make any difference. We will only know the emptiness of wrong expectations until we come to know and worship God in Jesus Christ. We find it comfortable to view the helpless infant in a manger. But we must not linger at the manger; rather we must look beyond the Cross to the empty tomb so that we can encounter a risen Lord! We must not stop with viewing the initial experience of Christ in this world or the first encounter of Christ in our lives, but we must seek to grow in a daily, personal relationship with him. We must not give up in pessimism when we do not achieve what we want in the world, but we must learn the peace that only Christ can give when we worship and acknowledge him as Lord.

Our expectations are just as wrong as the Israelites when we think God is going to do everything for us just because we think we are special. We have wrong expectations when we think we have to do everything for ourselves. An unnamed person summed up how we might avoid the emptiness of wrong expectations:

> Spin carefully
> spin prayerfully
> but leave the thread with God.

We must learn to work and pray in such a way that we encounter God in authentic worship. Then we need to leave the thread of our lives with God and entrust ourselves into the hands of his Son who gave his life for our salvation. To live apart from such a faith relationship is to give ourselves up to the emptiness of wrong expectations. We either seek to destroy the presence of God in the world or we come to worship him as Lord. There is no other choice. One way is filled with despair and wrong expectations. The other is filled with joy, hope, peace, love, and life!

Note

1. Frederick Buechner, *The Magnificent Defeat* (New York: The Seabury Press, 1969), p. 69.

11
The Literature of Preaching
William P. Tuck

1. Preaching to the Contemporary Mind

Abbey, Merrill R. *Preaching to the Contemporary Mind.* New York: Abingdon Press, 1963. 192 pp.

> (Begins with an examination of current attitudes and moods prevalant in the early sixties and then discusses four problems: secularism, freedom, the world crisis, and character crisis. The appendix suggests sermon starters to engage the contemporary mind in meaningful dialogue.)

Craddock, Fred B. *As One Without Authority.* Enid, Oklahoma: The Phillips University Press, 1971. 159 pp. Reprinted by Abingdon Press, 1979.

> (A statement of Craddock's understanding of preaching as inductive. He examines inductive preaching and its relationship to imagination, movement and unity of the sermon, the text, and structure.)

_____. *Overhearing the Gospel.* New York: Abingdon Press, 1978. 144 pp.

> (Lyman Beecher Lectures for 1978. A further development of his theory of inductive preaching built on insights from Sören Kierkegaard, the Danish theologian. A very challenging and original work.)

Forsyth, P. T. *Positive Preaching and the Modern Mind.* London: Independent Press, 1907. 258 pp. Reprinted by Baker Books, 1980.

> (Although quite old, still very helpful in its examination of the cross of Christ as central in any attempt to proclaim Christ.)

Mitchell, Henry H. *The Recovery of Preaching*. San Francisco: Harper and Row, 1977. 168 pp.

> (One of the most important books on preaching in recent years. Calls upon preachers to address not only the intellect but the total person in preaching. His concept of transconsciousness requires the preacher to speak out of one's own "depth" to the deep needs of others. He draws upon the strong black tradition in preaching for guidelines in how to accomplish this.)

Porteous, Alvin C. *Preaching to Suburban Captives*. Valley Forge: Judson Press, 1979, 125 pp.

> (Seeks to relate the gospel to suburban and city churches in their concern for the oppressed while at the same time addressing the needs of one's own people. He draws upon the theology of liberation to accomplish this goal. Five sermons on personhood, ecology, and so forth are offered as samples.)

Young, Robert D. *Religious Imagination: God's Gift to Prophets and Preachers*. Philadelphia: The Westminster Press, 1979. 176 pp.

> (Some original and perceptive ideas about preaching. Conceives the modern-day minister and others linked to prophets and seers of biblical times by unique creative insight into what God is doing. Designed to challenge the minister to bring out his own creativity.)

2. Preaching and Church Growth

Chaney, Charles L. and Ron S. Lewis. *Design for Church Growth*. Nashville: Broadman Press, 1977. 216 pp.

> (Presents principles for church growth and guidelines for ways to accomplish it. A companion workbook offers specific planning tools for implementing the book.)

Costas, Orlando. *The Church and Its Mission*. Wheaton: Tyndale House, 1974. 313 pp.

_____. *The Integrity of Mission: The Inner Life and Outreach of the Church*. New York: Harper & Row, 1979. 114 pp.

> (Challenges the church to indepth growth, life-style

growth, and numerical growth. He calls for an evangelistic atmosphere that will be evident in the sermons, prayers, and hymns.)

Fisher, Wallace E. *From Tradition to Mission*. New York: Abingdon Press, 1965. 208 pp.

(Based not on speculation about renewal in the church but the story of what one congregation, Holy Trinity Lutheran Church in Lancaster, Pennsylvania, actually did to be a more vital congregation in a metropolitan area.)

Hogue, C. B. *I Want My Church to Grow*. Nashville: Broadman Press, 1977. 160 pp.

(A good basic Baptist approach to church growth written by the former director of the evangelism section of the Home Mission Board of the Southern Baptist Convention. Very readable with definite guidelines.)

Hunter, George G., III. *The Contagious Congregation: Frontiers in Evangelism and Church Growth*. Nashville: Abingdon Press, 1979. 160 pp.

(Written by the director of evangelism for the United Methodists. Presents a helpful theological treatment with some very practical suggestions.)

McGavran, Donald. *Understanding Church Growth*. Grand Rapids: William B. Eerdmans, 1970. 382 pp.

(This is the classic, foundational book by the "father" of the church growth movement. This is the basic primer.)

Miles, Delos. *Church Growth: A Mighty River*. Nashville: Broadman Press, 1981. 167 pp.

(A good survey of the church growth movement. It deals not so much with actual principles as the history and development of the movement through the last twenty-five years.)

Miller, Calvin. *A View from the Fields*. Nashville: Broadman Press, 1978. 136 pp.

(A view of how one pastor did church growth in his Omaha community. Gives his dreaming; planning; and theological, psychological, and sociological approach to church growth. A practical and helpful source from a pastor who knows church growth both as theory and practice.)

Raines, Robert A. *New Life in the Church*. New York: Harper & Row, 1961. 155 pp.

(Written by a former pastor of Aldersgate Methodist Church in Cleveland, Ohio, who led his congregation in an exciting recovery of its sense of mission in converting and transforming society. Many practical suggestions for revitalizing the lay ministry.)

Schuller, Robert H. *Your Church Has Real Possibilities*. Glendale, California: G/L Publications, 1974. 179 pp.

(Based on the actual workshop and experience of Robert Schuller at the Garden Grove Community Church. Presents clearly the pragmatics of church growth.)

Wagner, C. Peter. *Your Church Can Grow*. Glendale, California: G/L Publications, 1976. 176 pp.

(Presents seven vital signs of a healthy church.)

3. Confessional Preaching

Claypool, John R. *The Preaching Event*. Waco, Texas: Word Books, 1980. 139 pp.

(The Lyman Beecher Lectures for 1979. Here the author sets forth his theory of confessional preaching. Drawing upon the incarnational model made flesh in the person of Jesus, he denotes that the word must become flesh in the life of the preacher. Preaching is described as "event" because words are a form of deed. To be effective the preacher must share honestly out of his own struggles.)

_____. *Tracks of a Fellow Struggler: How to Handle Grief*. Waco, Texas. Word Books, 1974. 104 pp.

(A collection of four sermons dealing with the grief process which he and his family experienced during the illness and death of his daughter. Here the author shares both struggles and light that come through human tragedy.)

Jourard, Sidney M. *The Transparent Self*. New York: Van Nostrand Reinhold Co., 1971. 250 pp.

(A challenge to reveal one's authentic self rather than hiding or misrepresenting one's real feelings. The self-disclosure which the author commends has many solid suggestions for preaching.)

Nouwen, Henri J. M. *Creative Ministry.* Garden City, New York: Doubleday & Co., Inc., 1971. 119 pp.

(Chapter 2, "Beyond the Retelling of the Story," is a summons for the preacher to assist persons in their ongoing struggle of becoming. The preacher is challenged to be willing to lay himself and his own suffering and hope available to others so they can also find their way.)

_____. *The Wounded Healer: Ministry in Contemporary Society.* Garden City, New York: Doubleday & Co., 1972. 104 pp.

(Explores the suffering of contemporary persons who are psychologically wounded by lack of hope, by loneliness, by the predicament of rootlessness. The minister is able to help others deal with these problems as he/she is willing to go beyond the professional role and be open as a fellow human being with his/her own wounds and suffering.)

Quoist, Michel. *Prayers.* New York: Avon, 1975. 179 pp.

(This collection of personal prayers has become a classic. These prayers reveal the most intimate and personal struggles of one who talked with God about the daily events of his life. These prayers are compelling windows into the soul of one man's private moments with God.)

Raines, Robert A. *Lord, Could You Make It a Little Better?* Waco, Texas: Word Books, 1972. 147 pp.

(Prayers in which the author has expressed the deep yearnings of his deepest needs and feelings. Poetic at times, these prayers arise and speak to the basic senses within us.)

_____. *To Kiss the Joy.* Waco, Texas: Word Books, 1973. 151 pp.

(Sermons based on personal thoughts and feelings regarding the painful process of growth. Thoughtful in its call to sense the amazing grace of God which accepts us all as we are.)

4. Preaching the Parables
          A. Special Studies on the Parables

Bailey, Kenneth E. *Through Peasant Eyes.* Grand Rapids: William B. Eerdmans, Co., 1980. 187 pp.

> (Perceives parables as dramatic forms of theological language that press the listeners to respond. He examines the literary structure and cultural milieu of ten parables.)

Barclay, William. *And Jesus Said: A Handbook on the Parables of Jesus.* Philadelphia: The Westminster Press, 1970. 224 pp.

> (Examines briefly thirty-four parables. The theme of each parable is related in light of the customs of the biblical world, and its contemporary message is stated in a clear way.)

Buttrick, George A. *The Parables of Jesus.* New York: Harper & Row, 1928. Baker Books Reprint. 274 pp.

> (Although quite old, still offers helpful preaching and teaching suggestions on forty-four parables.)

Dodd, C. H. *The Parables of the Kingdom.* New York: Charles Scribner's Sons, 1938. Revised edition 1961. 176 pp.

> (Addressed the meaning of the parables and their application for the audience to which Jesus originally uttered them. The *Sitz im Leben* must be known before we can interpret them for today. This book opened a new era in the study of parables.)

Hunter, Archibald M. *Interpreting the Parables.* Philadelphia: The Westminster Press, 1960. 126 pp.

_____. *The Parables Then and Now.* Philadelphia: The Westminster Press, 1971.

> (Popular treatments of a number of parables examining them in their original meaning and relevance for today.)

Jeremias, Joachim. *The Parables of Jesus.* London: SCM Press, 1954. 178 pp. There is a revised issue of this work in which the Greek words have been translated under the title *Rediscover-*

ing the Parables, New York: Charles Scribner's Sons, 1966. 191 pp.

(Jeremias carried forward systematically and in greater detail the work which Dodd began in a preliminary way. He tried to ascertain the actual words of Jesus in the parables.)

Jones, Peter Rhea. *The Teaching of the Parables.* Nashville: Broadman Press, 1982. 263 pp.

(In three chapters Jones surveys the past and recent interpretations of the parables; examines the nature of parables as literary form, historical event, and hermeneutical; and suggests some clear characteristics of parables as literary art forms. In eleven other chapters, he examines selected parables with depth and insight seeking to discern their original intent. In every chapter he offers suggestions for applying the meaning of the parables for today. An excellent resource for the pastor and teacher.)

Stein, Robert H. *An Introduction to the Parables of Jesus.* Philadelphia: The Westminster Press, 1981. 180 pp.

(A helpful source on updating parable studies from the past to the present.)

Via, Dan Otto, Jr. *The Parables.* Philadelphia: Fortress Press, 1967. 217 pp.

(An examination of the parables in dialogue with aesthetic criticism. The parables are viewed as vehicles meant to bring decision.)

B. Sermon Books on the Parables

Brunner, Emil. *Sowing and Reaping.* Richmond: John Knox Press, 1964. 91 pp.

(A theologian offers some interesting sermons on several parables.)

Hamilton, J. Wallace. *Horns and Halos in Human Nature.* Westwood, N.Y.: Fleming H. Revell Co., 1954. 173 pp.

(Fourteen sermons on the parable of the Prodigal Son. Good suggestions for series.)

Kennedy, Gerald. *The Parables: Sermons on the Stories Jesus Told.* New York: Harper & Row, 1960. 213 pp.
> (Fresh and stimulating treatment of most of the New Testament parables.)

Ogilvie, Lloyd John. *Autobiography of God.* Glendale, California: Ragal Books, 1979. 320 pp.
> (In spite of the title, one will find some very helpful, practical, and meaningful sermons in this collection. Ogilvie takes the text seriously most of the time and relates the teaching of the parable to meet the needs of people today.)

Thielicke, Helmut. *The Waiting Father: Sermons on the Parables of Jesus.* New York: Harper & Brothers, 1959. 192 pp.
> (Masterpieces by a leading theologian. Sixteen parables are treated.)

Weatherhead, Leslie D. *In Quest of a Kingdom.* New York: Abingdon Press, 1944. 268 pp.
> (A popular treatment with numerous illustrative suggestions.)

5. Ethical Dimensions of Preaching

Braidfoot, Larry, (editor). "Preaching on Ethical Issues," *Light.* A bimonthly bulletin, published by the Christian Life Commission of the Southern Baptist Convention. December, 1981. 16 pp.
> (Articles by William Pinson, Jr. "Biblical and Historical Models"; Cecil Sherman, "Preparations, Delivery and Reaction"; Don B. Harbuck, "In the Context of the Pastor's Total Ministry." Very helpful.)

Coffin, William Sloane. *The Courage to Love.* San Francisco: Harper & Row, 1982. 100 pp.
> (Sermons by the current Riverside preacher on significant crucial issues of our time such as abortion, homosexuality, the arms race, burnout, and so forth.)

Cox, James W. (editor). *The Twentieth Century Pulpit.* Vol. II.

Nashville: Abingdon Press, 1981. 238 pp.

(Contemporary preachers such as John Claypool, Elizabeth Achtemeier, John Fry, Jürgen Moltmann speak on social and ethical issues confronting today's world.)

Furnish, Victor Paul. *The Moral Teachings of Paul.* Nashville: Abingdon Press, 1979. 141 pp.

(A popular treatment of such issues as the following: negative uses of the Bible, sex, marriage and divorce, homosexuality, women in the church, and Christians and the civil authorities. Very useful. Helpful in church discussion groups.)

Gonzales, Justo L. and Catherine. *Liberation Preaching: The Pulpit and the Oppressed.* Nashville: Abingdon Press, 1980. 127 pp.

(Drawing on liberation theology, the authors set forth the concepts, dynamics, methods, and forms to enable preachers to speak to the needs of the powerless in the world. They offer guidance regarding hearing and interpreting the text and a summons to actual involvement in the process of liberation.)

Jersild, Paul T. and Dale A. Johnson (editors). *Moral Issues and Christian Purpose.* New York: Holt, Rinehart, and Winston, 1976. 410 pp.

(A collection of readings from a varied group like John Bennett, Helmut Thielicke, James Baldwin, Will Campbell, Rosemary Ruether, Carlyle Marney, and Roger Shinn on such issues as morality, sexuality, race, women's movement, homosexuality, population, nuclear war, abortion, and euthanasia. A very thorough and many-sided approach.)

Simmons, Paul D. (editor). *Issues in Christian Ethics.* Nashville: Broadman Press, 1980. 260 pp.

(Presents a method and scope of Christian ethics and then deals with current issues like the future of the family, women's liberation, bioethics, ecology, peace, liberation movement, political action and the black church, and social justice. A scholarly and readable source which will challenge one's preaching on these issues.)

Thielicke, Helmut. *Theological Ethics.* Philadelphia: Fortress Press, 1966. c. 2000 pp. (3 volumes).

(The theological foundation for Thielicke's preaching. Attempts to show that preaching is vitally concerned with the secular problems and issues of modern life. A classical, scholarly treatment of theological ethics.)

Yoder, John Howard. *The Politics of Jesus.* Grand Rapids: William B. Eerdmans, Co., 1972. 260 pp.

(A position of Christian pacifism based on a careful studying of the Gospel text, especially Luke.)

6. Legitimate Shortcuts in Sermon Preparation

Achtemeier, Elizabeth, Gerhard Krodel and Charles P. Price (editors). *Proclamation.* Series B. Philadelphia: Fortress Press, 1981. c. 64 pp.

(Eight volumes providing aids for interpreting the Scripture and homiletic suggestions for the appointed common lectionary lessons of the church year. Separate volumes on Advent-Christmas, Epiphany, Lent, Holy Week, Easter, Pentecost, and lesser festivals. Writers such as Fred Craddock, Ernest Saunders, Urban Holmes wrote the material.)

Cox, James W. (editor). *The Ministers Manual.* 1983 Edition. San Francisco: Harper & Row, 1982. 280 pp.

(Guidance for worship service, special occasions, sermon outlines, prayers, resources for funerals, communion, and other services, as well as stories for children, illustrations, and suggestions for preaching themes, special days, and so forth.)

_____. (editor). *Pulpit Digest.* Jackson, Mississippi.

(Published six times a year. Offers sermons, preaching resources, illustrations, and other aids for sermon preparation.)

Crabtree, T. T. (editor). *The Zondervan 1983 Pastor's Annual*. Grand Rapids: Zondervan Publishing House, 1982. 383 pp.

> (Suggests a planned preaching program for every Sunday of the year. Provides communion helps, funeral messages, wedding ceremonies, prayers, messages for children and adults, and other suggestions.)

Craddock, Fred B. *John Knox Preaching Guides*. Atlanta: John Knox Press, 1982. 149 pp.

> (This is one volume of a very useful series which offers valuable guides to preaching and pastoral application of biblical passages based on sound exegesis. Many noted scholars have made fine contributions to this helpful series of preaching guides.)

Hightower, James E., Jr. (editor). *Proclaim*. Published quarterly by The Sunday School Board of the Southern Baptist Convention, Nashville, Tennessee.

> (A resource journal to help the pastor in preaching and worship. Suggests sermon ideas, illustrations, resources for special occasions, and articles on pulpit performance.)

Kennedy, Gerald, (Compiler). *A Reader's Notebook*. New York: Harper & Brothers, 1953. 340 pp.

> (A collection of quotations and illustrations listed by topics. He has two other published notebooks.)

Marshall, Alfred. *The Interlinear Greek-English New Testament*. London: Samuel Bagster & Sons, 1959. 1027 pp.

> (Helpful in getting the literal translation of a passage of Scripture.)

Pearce, J. Winston. *Planning Your Preaching*. Nashville: Broadman Press, 1967. 197 pp.

> (Long-range planning of preaching around such emphases as the Christian year, preaching through the Bible, meeting people's needs, denominational calendar, evangelistic purposes, baptism, and the Lord's Supper.)

Steel, David. *Preaching Through the Year*. Atlanta: John Knox Press, 1980. 170 pp.

> (Offers suggestions for text, reference, and sermon outlines

for liturgical seasons plus special days and observances. Helpful and stimulating.)

Wallis, Charles L. (editor). *Speakers Resources from Contemporary Literature*. New York: Harper & Row, 1965. 282 pp.

(Extracts from contemporary narrative and dramatic literature. 898 selections from 350 major works by 200 novelists and dramatists.)

7. Coordinating Preaching with Church Objectives

(The books by Achtemeier, *et al*, Pearce, Steel, and Wallis may also be useful under this section.)

Anderson, James D. and Ezra Earl Jones. *The Management of Ministry*. San Francisco: Harper & Row, 1978. 202 pp.

(Identifies six different types of churches based on their community (open country to those in the urban central business districts of major cities) and notes the five distinct phases in its life. Suggested creative responses to meet the spiritual needs are cited. Offers guidance for a church to define its own priorities and identify the best means of attaining them.)

Fisher, Wallace E. *A New Climate For Stewardship*. Nashville: Abingdon Press, 1976. 127 pp.

(A resource for a congregation to determine its personal, social, and congregational priorities in the light of a biblical understanding of stewardship.)

Lindgren, Alvin J. *Foundations for Purposeful Church Administration*. Nashville: Abingdon Press, 1965. 302 pp.

(Not a book about church administration but a guiding statement for church administrators. Focuses on what church administration is, the foundation on which it rests, and the prerequisites for leadership in this field. This book deals with the nature and mission of the church, building a spiritual foundation through worship and study, comprehensive planning, equipping lay persons for leadership and service, and other items.)

Oates, Wayne E. *The Christian Pastor*. Third Edition, Philadelphia:

The Westminster Press, 1982. 298 pp.

(A classic on the pastor's ministry, showing the pastoral task and methods. This edition includes up-to-date research on the role of the pastor in contemporary life. The author makes use of recent psychological interpretations and at the same time preserves the biblical and theological emphasis of earlier editions.)

Switzer, David K. *Pastor, Preacher, Person: Developing a Pastoral Ministry in Depth.* Nashville: Abingdon, 1979. 144 pp.

(A practical book which presents methods for using the insights gained in pastoral care to help integrate the personal concerns of a minister with his professional goals. Suggests some helpful ingredients in meaningful preaching to address the real needs of people.)

Willimon, William H. *Integrative Preaching: The Pulpit at the Center.* Nashville: Abingdon Press, 1981. 110 pp.

(The preaching ministry is examined in relation to other pastoral functions, such as administration, counseling, study visitation, and teaching. He shows how these strengthen and inform the pulpit ministry.)

8. Narrative Preaching

Brown, David M. *Dramatic Narrative in Preaching.* Valley Forge: Judson Press, 1981. 96 pp.

(An examination of the methodology of the preaching narrative from its inception to its delivery. The reader is told how to investigate a character and write the story to hold interest. Five narrative sample sermons are given. A helpful bibliography is included.)

Lowry, Eugene L. *The Homiletical Plot: The Sermon as Narrative Art Form.* Atlanta: John Knox, 1980. 100 pp.

(A practical resource for a variety of storytelling methods, techniques, anecdotes, metaphors, story form, and dialogues.)

Jensen, Richard A. *Telling the Story: Variety and Imagination in*

Preaching. Minneapolis: Augsburg Publishing House, 1980. 189 pp.

(A trained theologian presents three types of preaching: the didactic sermon, the proclamatory sermon, and the story sermon. He gives a summary and charateristic of each type and then illustrates each type with one or more sermons. His chapter on story preaching provides some excellent guidelines for the preacher on "how to do it.")

McClendon, James Wm. *Biography as Theology: How Life Stories Can Remake Today's Theology*. Nashville: Abingdon Press, 1974. 224 pp.

(Proposes that character is based on convictions, and theology has to do basically with convictions. Examines Dag Hammarskjöld, Martin Luther King, Jr., Clarence Jordan, and Charles Ives to establish his theory.)

McEachern, Alton H. *Proclaim the Gospel*. Nashville: Convention Press, 1975. 144 pp.

(A section on dramatic monologue preaching is found on pages 61-65. Suggestions for preparation, delivery, and sources are offered here.)

Reid, John Calvin. *We Knew Jesus*. Grand Rapids: Wm. B. Eerdmans Publishing Co., 1954. 148 pp.

(Twelve sermons delivered from the perspective of various contemporaries of Jesus and their reaction to him. Imaginative examples of narrative preaching.)

Sanders, James A. *God Has a Story, Too: Sermons in Context*. Philadelphia: Fortress Press, 1979. 145 pp.

(The hermeneutical techniques which he suggests are dynamic analogy, the concept of memory or re-presentation today of tension and resolution in the biblical accounts as mirrors for morality. He gives nine sermons as examples of his principles.)

Speakman, Frederick B. *God and Jack Wilson*. Westwood: Fleming H. Revell Co., 1955. 125 pp.

(Narrative sermons delivered by an imaginary preacher in

a sort of autobiographical way. Two other books by the same author, *The Salty Tang* and *Love Is Something You Do*, are also very helpful.)

Steimle, Edmund A., Morris J. Niedenthal, and Charles L. Rice. *Preaching the Story.* Philadelphia: Fortress Press, 1980. 198 pp.

(A useful introduction to preaching as "shared story." Suggestions are offered on how to move from the Story to our story.)

Thompson, William D. and Gordon C. Bennett. *Dialogue Preaching: The Shared Sermon.* Valley Forge: The Judson Press, 1969. 158 pp.

(The authors analyze the nature, varieties, and functions of dialogue preaching. Eight dialogue sermons are offered as examples of this preaching method.)

Troeger, Thomas H. *Creating Fresh Images for Preaching.* Valley Forge: Judson Press, 1982. 141 pp.

(A creative and stimulating source for fresh approaches to sermon preparation. A book to sharpen the imagination and push the creative button to set the preacher free from the predictable pattern of sermonizing.)

9. Preaching in the Context of Crises

Bailey, Robert W. *The Minister and Grief.* New York: Hawthorn Books, Inc., 1976. 114 pp. Reprinted by Zondervan Press, 1980, under the title *Ministering to the Grieving.*

(A very practical book in guiding ministers to understand his own attitude toward grief and death, and provides resources for ministering to the dying, and grieving. Very helpful resources for funerals.)

Jackson, Edgar N. *How to Preach to People's Needs.* Grand Rapids: Baker Book House, 1970. 191 pp.

(Provides suggestions for preaching to sixteen different needs such as guilt-laden, sorrow-filled, defeated, and problem drinkers.)

Kushner, Harold S. *When Bad Things Happen to Good People.* New

York: Schocken Books, 1981. 149 pp.

(A popular book directed to those who have been hurt by life, death, illness, injury, rejection, or disappointment. An attempt to affirm the goodness of God in the difficult times of pain and tears.)

Oates, Wayne E. *Pastoral Care and Counseling in Grief and Separation.* Philadelphia: Fortress Press, 1976. 86 pp.

(Offers resources for the pastor in ministering to the bereaved. Focuses realistically upon the pastor's resources and limitations in caring for and counseling in grief experiences.)

Teikmanis, Arthur L. *Preaching and Pastoral Care.* Philadelphia: Fortress Press, 1968. 144 pp.

(Shows how the insights from pastoral counseling can be employed meaningfully in preaching. Offers guidance during the crises of life to those who are spiritually isolated by anxiety, loneliness, unforgiveness, hatred. Focuses also on community problems which are of deep concern to our church people.)

Tuck, William P. *Facing Grief and Death.* Nashville: Broadman Press, 1975. 153 pp.

(Practical guidelines for helping persons face their fear of death, learning how to meet grief, helping a friend in grief, noting death and the meaning of life, and facing the mystery of death. In the second part of the book a physician, a lawyer, and a funeral director deal with questions people usually raise to them regarding death.)

Westberg, Granger E. *Good Grief: A Constructive Approach to the Problem of Loss.* Philadelphia: Fortress Press, 1962. 57 pp.

(Ten stages of grief are presented in a clear, straightforward manner.)

10. Preaching in the Context of Worship

Bailey, Robert W. *New Ways in Christian Worship.* Nashville: Broadman Press, 1981. 164 pp.

(Offers guidance in understanding worship, planning, and

evaluating worship. Suggestions are presented for worship
on twenty special days like Advent, Race Relations Sunday,
Christian Home Week, and Labor Day. Very practical and
creative.)

Barry, James C. and Jack Gulledge (comp. & editor). *Ideas for
Effective Worship Services.* Nashville: Convention Press, 1977.
84 pp.

(A resource to help pastors and other staff plan, conduct,
and evaluate worship services. Experienced ministers
share suggestions about how to improve music, prayers,
preaching, the order of the services, baptism, Lord's
Supper lay involvement, and other dimensions in worship.)

Hoon, Paul Waitman. *The Integrity of Worship: Ecumenical and
Pastoral Studies in Liturgical Theology.* Nashville: Abingdon
Press, 1971. 363 pp.

(A theology of liturgy which is both theoretical and practical. A scholarly treatment which puts worship at the
center of the church's life.)

Killinger, John. *How to Enrich Your Worship.* Nashville: Abingdon
Press, 1977.

(Four cassette tapes on the following areas of worship: the
importance of worship, worship and prayer, using the
Scriptures, the sermon, communion, music, commitment,
and finally a potpourri of suggestions. A leader's guide is
furnished with a number of worship aids.)

Segler, Franklin M. *Christian Worship: Its Theology and Practice.*
Nashville: Broadman Press, 1967. 245 pp.

(Explores the meaning of worship, the means of expressing
worship, and ways of planning and conducting worship.
Moves from the biblical foundations of worship to the week
by week experience of leading worship.)

Wainwright, Geoffrey. *Doxology: The Praise of God in Worship,
Doctrine, and Life.* New York: Oxford University Press, 1980.
609 pp.

(A major work that breaks new ground by presenting a

systematic theology from the angle of worship. Not easy reading but one well worth the effort.)

White, James F. *Introduction to Christian Worship*. Nashville: Abingdon Press, 1980. 288 pp.

(A comprehensive survey of Christian worship which focuses on its meaning and practice. Historical, theological, and pastoral dimensions of Christian worship are noted throughout this study.)

_____. *New Forms of Worship*. Nashville: Abingdon Press, 1971. 222 pp.

(Traces the history of Christian liturgy and examines the basic elements, including preaching, which constitute worship.)

Willimon, William H. *Worship as Pastoral Care*. Nashville: Abingdon Press, 1979. 237 pp.

(Drawing on the insights of pastoral psychology and pastoral care, the author shows how worship is enriched by them and how worship supports them. He examines four acts of worship: the funeral, the wedding, baptism, and the Lord's Supper to show the way pastoral care is taking place through these services of worship.)

Biographical Sketches

Robert W. Bailey is the pastor of the Southside Baptist Church of Birmingham, Alabama. He holds the B.A. from Carson-Newman College and the B.D. and S.T.D. from The Southern Baptist Theological Seminary. He was pastor in Kentucky and North Carolina before going to Alabama. He is the author of *The Minister and Grief, God's Questions and Answers, New Ways in Christian Worship, The Joy of Discipleship,* and *Coping with Stress in the Minister's Home*. He has contributed to many other publications of the Baptist Sunday School Board. He has lectured on preaching and congregational worship in state conferences and has been a conference leader for the Sunday School Board in other areas of pastoral work.

James C. Barry is a pastoral consultant in the Church Administration Department of the Baptist Sunday School Board. He is a native of Kentucky and holds the B.A. from Western Kentucky University. He has the B.D., Th.M., and Ph.D. from The Southern Baptist Theological Seminary. He was a pastor in Kentucky and Virginia for ten years before going to the Board. Preaching and congregational worship are the two areas of primary responsibility, but he has been a frequent speaker in state and national conferences in all areas related to pastors. He has planned and directed five national conferences on preaching and has helped to plan and conduct one or more state conferences on preaching in every state convention but two. He is a member of the Academy of Homiletics. He compiled the books *Preaching People-to-People, Ideas for Effective Worship Services,* and *Award Winning Sermons, Volume 1, Volume 2, Volume 3,* and *Volume 4.*

Lavonn D. Brown is the pastor of the First Baptist Church of Norman, Oklahoma. He has the B.A. from Oklahoma Baptist University and the B.D. and Th.D. from Southwestern Baptist Theological Seminary. He served as pastor of other churches in Oklahoma and Texas before going to

220

Norman. He has served on executive boards for institutions and groups in Oklahoma and the Southern Baptist Convention, including Oklahoma Baptist University, The Southern Baptist Theological Seminary, the General Convention of Oklahoma—of which he served as president. He has represented both his state and convention on the Committee on Boards. He delivered lectures on preaching at both Southern and Southwestern seminaries and at the Southern Baptist Seminary in Rio de Janeiro, Brazil. Also, he has lectured on preaching at national and state conferences on preaching. He has written *Salvation in Our Time, Youth Affirm: The Doctrine of Salvation, Truths That Make a Difference*, and contributed to *Award Winning Sermons.*

John R. Claypool is on the pastoral team of the Second Baptist Church of Lubbock, Texas. He holds the B.A. from Baylor University and the B.D. and Th.D. from The Southern Baptist Theological Seminary. Two honorary degrees have been received: the D.D. from Georgetown College and the L.L.D. from Baylor University. Further study has been done at Princeton, Yale, Union of New York, Regent's Park of London, Perkins of Dallas, Ecumenical Institute of Israel, Jungian Institute of Zurich, and others. He brought the Hester Lectures on Preaching at both Midwestern and Golden Gate seminaries, the Adams Lectures on Preaching at Southeastern, and the Mullins Lectures on Preaching at Southern Seminary. In 1979 he brought the Lyman Beecher Lectures on Preaching at Yale. These were published under the title of *The Preaching Event*. He has been a member of the executive board of many religious and civic groups in Kentucky, Mississippi, Louisiana, and Texas, as well as the Southern Baptist Convention.

J. Truett Gannon is the pastor of the Smoke Rise Baptist Church in Stone Mountain, Georgia. He holds the B.A. from Mercer University and the B.D. and D. Min. from Southeastern Baptist Theological Seminary. He served as pastor in North Carolina and Louisiana before going to Georgia. He has served on the executive boards for Mercer University, Louisiana Baptist College, Midwestern Baptist Theological Seminary, the Brotherhood Commission of the Southern Baptist Convention, the Georgia Baptist Convention, and the Georgia Baptist Hospital Commission. He has held leadership roles with the Georgia Baptist Convention, the Atlanta Baptist Pastors' Conference, and with the Mercer and Southeastern Seminary alumni groups. He has been a speaker for state and national conventions.

William E. Hull is the pastor of the First Baptist Church of Shreveport, Louisiana. He has the B.A. from Samford University, the M.Div. and Ph.D. from The Southern Baptist Theological Seminary, and advanced study at University of Gottingen, Germany, and Harvard University. He was professor of New Testament, dean, and provost at the Southern Seminary prior to going to Shreveport. He has served as visiting professor at the Baptist Theological Seminary, Ruschlikon, Switzerland; Louisiana State University School of Medicine; and the Nigerian Baptist Theological Seminary. He has served on various executive boards and committees for the state of Louisiana, the Southern Baptist Convention, and the Baptist World Alliance. He has been speaker for the "Baptist Hour" and on programs for the Baptist World Alliance, the Southern Baptist Convention, and for many other state and national conventions. He is author of *The Gospel of John;* "John," *Broadman Bible Commentary*, Volume 9, *The Bible, Beyond the Barriers, Love in Four Dimensions*, and has contributed to many other books and journals.

Peter Rhea Jones is the pastor of the First Baptist Church of Decatur, Georgia. He holds the B.A. from Union University, the M.A. from University of Mississippi, the Th.M. from Princeton Theological Seminary, and the M.Div. and Ph.D. from The Southern Baptist Theological Seminary. Graduate work has been done at Cambridge University. He served as associate professor of New Testament at Southern before going to Georgia, during which time he was in constant demand as an interim pastor. He has brought numerous biblical lectures to pastors' conferences, conventions, and divinity school, such as Vanderbilt University and Southeastern Baptist Theological Seminary. He is author of *The Teaching of the Parables* and has written several articles for the *Review and Expositor* and other scholarly journals. He writes regularly for curriculum publications.

C. David Matthews is the pastor of the First Baptist Church of Greenville, South Carolina. He holds the B.A. from Baylor University and the B.D. and Th.D. from Southwestern Baptist Theological Seminary. He served as pastor in Oklahoma and Texas before going to South Carolina. He is the author of *Prayer Meeting Resources, Volume 2*, two musical compositions, plus sermons and articles for several Sunday School Board publications. He has served on the executive boards for Baylor University, the Baptist General Convention of Texas, the Christian Life Commission of Texas and the Southern Baptist Convention, the South Carolina Baptist Convention, and the Baptist World Alliance.

Alton H. McEachern is the pastor of the First Baptist Church of Greensboro, North Carolina. He holds the B.A. from Mercer University and the M.Div., Th.M., and D.Min. from The Southern Baptist Theological Seminary. He has done graduate work at University of Glasgow, Scotland, and Mansfield College, Oxford. He has served as adjunct professor of preaching at Southern and Midwestern seminaries and as visiting professor at Southeastern and Nigerian Baptist seminaries. He was pastor in West Virginia and Kentucky before going to North Carolina. He is author of *Proclaim the Gospel, Here at Thy Table, Lord, Growing Disciples Through Preaching, Set Apart for Service, Psalms* in Layman's Bible Book Commentary, and *A Pattern for Prayer* and has contributed to other publications. He has been a member of the executive boards of Baptists in Ohio, Kentucky, and North Carolina, and on the board of trustees for Campbellsville College and Wake Forest University.

Calvin Miller is the pastor of the Westside Baptist Church in Omaha, Nebraska. He holds the B.S. from Oklahoma Baptist University and the M.Div. and D.Min. from Midwestern Baptist Theological Seminary. He is the author of fifteen books of popular theology and inspiration. His trilogy on *The Singer, The Song,* and *The Finale* provides a poetic interpretation of the gospel story. They have been on the best-seller lists and have been published in three foreign countries. Two fantasy fiction books *The Guardians of Singreale* and *Star Riders of Ren* are recent publications. *A View from the Fields* from Broadman Press is on church growth. He is a frequent speaker at national and state meetings, particularly with youth and college audiences.

J. Altus Newell is the pastor of the First Baptist Church of Opelika, Alabama. He holds the B.A. from Mississippi College and the M.Div. and Ph.D. from The Southern Baptist Theological Seminary. He studied at the University of Bonn as Rotary Foundation Fellow. He served as visiting professor in preaching at Southern. He was a pastor in Kentucky before going to Alabama. He has lectured at state conferences on preaching and on congregation worship. He contributed to *Award Winning Sermons* and has written for several Baptist Sunday School Board publications. He has served on various executive committees and boards for the Kentucky Baptist Convention, The Southern Baptist Theological Seminary, and the Southern Baptist Convention.

Cecil E. Sherman is the pastor of the First Baptist Church of Asheville, North Carolina. He holds the B.A. from Baylor University, the B.D. and Th.D. from Southwestern Baptist Theological Seminary, and the Th.M. from Princeton Theological Seminary. He held pastorates in Georgia and Texas before going to North Carolina. He is the author of *Modern Myths* from Broadman Press and contributed to *Award Winning Sermons.* He has written for other Baptist Sunday School Board publications. He has been president of the North Carolina Baptist Convention on two occasions, trustee of Meredith college, chairman of the Christian Life Commission of the Southern Baptist Convention, and member of other boards and commissions in his state.

William P. Tuck is the pastor of the Saint Matthews Baptist Church of Louisville, Kentucky. He received the B.A. from University of Richmond, the B.D. and Th.M. from Southeastern Baptist Theological Seminary, and the Th.D. from the New Orleans Baptist Theological Seminary. He has the D.D. from the University of Richmond. He was professor of Christian preaching at Southern before going to the Saint Matthews church. Prior to that he was pastor in Louisiana and Virginia. He is a member of the American Academy of Religion and of the Academy of Homiletics. He is author of *Facing Grief and Death, The Struggle for Meaning,* and *Knowing God: Religious Knowledge in the Theology of John Baillie.* He has contributed to other books and theological journals with material on preaching. He is a frequent curriculum writer for the Sunday School Board. He has been a speaker and conference leader at state and national meetings.